THE RANDOM HOUSE ACHIEVEMENT PROGRAM IN COMPREHENSION

Reading Consultant: TOM WOLPERT

Random House School Division

CONTENTS

Unit 1 • Decoding Words

Unit 2 • Understanding Words

Unit 3 • Understanding Sentences

Unit 4 • Understanding Selections

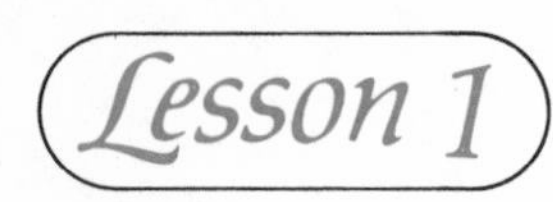

CONSONANTS / READING WORDS IN CONTEXT

YOU KNOW

- Letters stand for sounds.
- Two letters together can stand for one sound.
- Different letters can stand for the same sound.

Say the word that names each picture.

Name the picture. Draw a line to the letter or letters that stand for the sound you hear at the end of the picture name.

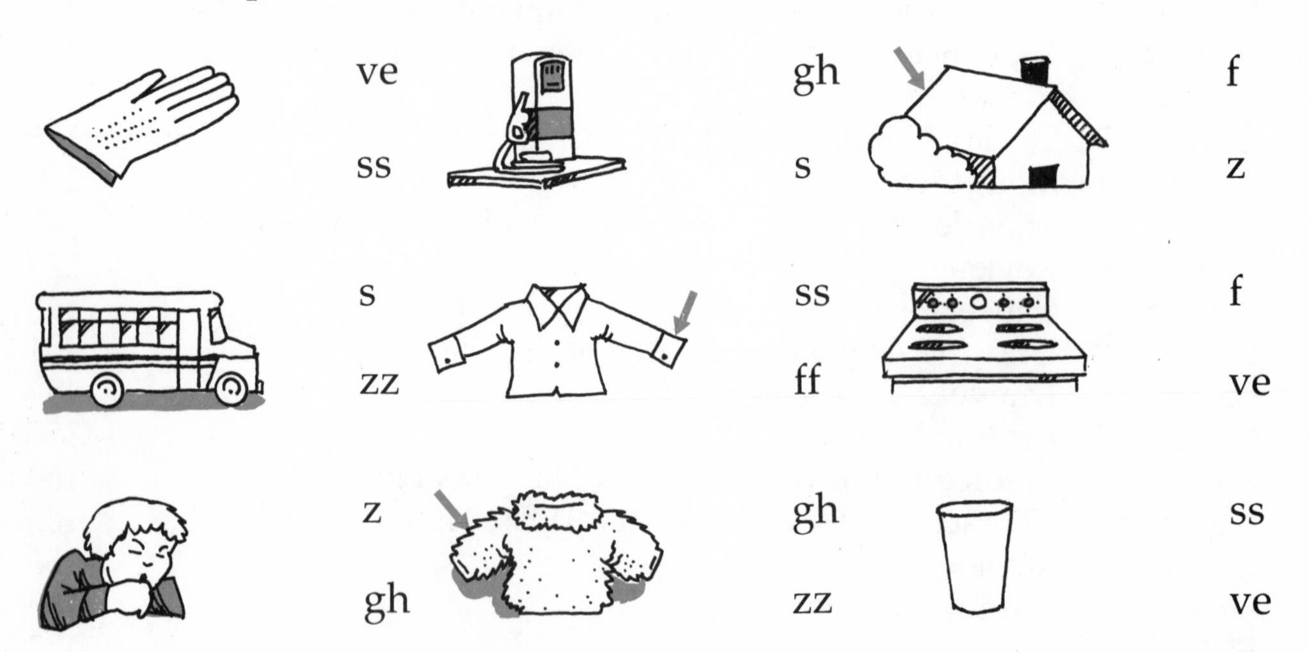

 Consonant sound-letter correspondences: final /f/ *f, ff, gh,* /s/ *s, ss,* /v/ *ve,* /z/ *z, zz;* using consonant sounds to decode words

USING WHAT YOU KNOW

Look at the letters in color. Knowing the sounds the letters stand for helps you read the words.

Here are some of the questions asked on the Quiz Whiz show. Read each question. Draw a line from the question to the answer.

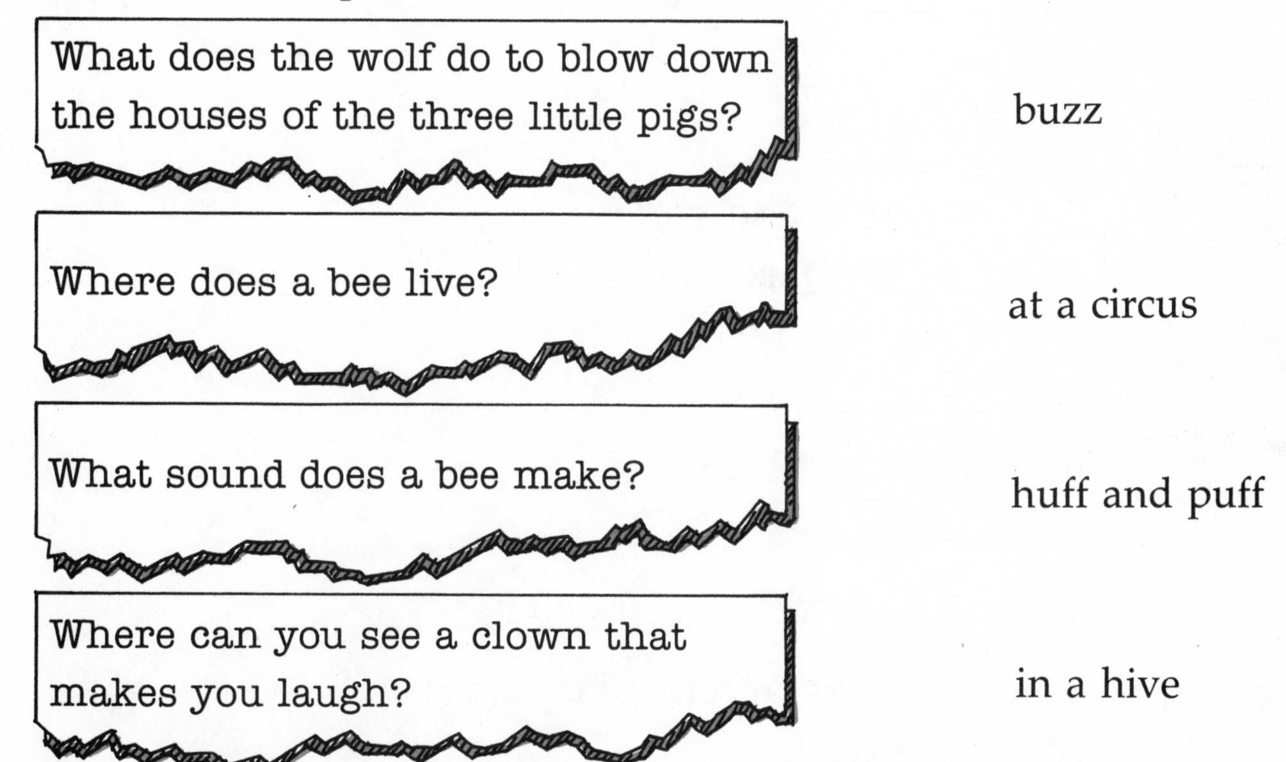

WHILE YOU READ

Use what you know about the sounds for letters to help you read new words.

Tess and Dave were on the Quiz Whiz show.

The man asked, "Where does a bear live?"

Dave gave a buzz. "In a cave," he said.

"Right!" said the man. "Now, here is a tough question. Name two green things with names that end with the same sound as <u>guess</u>.

Tess buzzed. "Grass and moss," she said.

"Right!" said the man. "You are even now. Answer the next question and you will be the Quiz Whiz! Just buzz on and off. What is in a school but never sits in a class?"

Tess buzzed first. "A fish," she said.

"Right! You are the Quiz Whiz!" said the man.

AFTER YOU READ

A. Fill in the circle for the answer.

1. Tess became the Quiz Whiz because she

○ went to school

○ had two right answers

○ knew where a bear lives

2. At the end, Tess was

○ wrong ○ sad ○ proud

B. Write some questions on cards. Play Quiz Whiz with your friends.

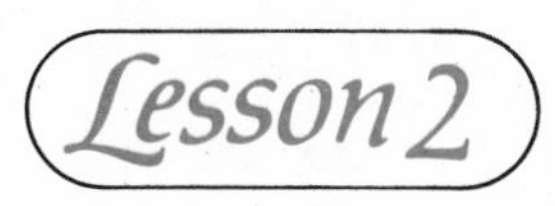

CONSONANTS / READING WORDS IN CONTEXT

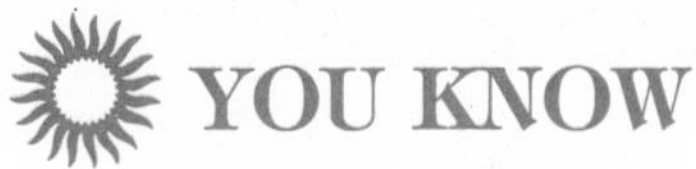

- Letters stand for sounds.
- Some letters stand for more than one sound.
- Different letters can stand for the same sound.

Say the word that names each picture.

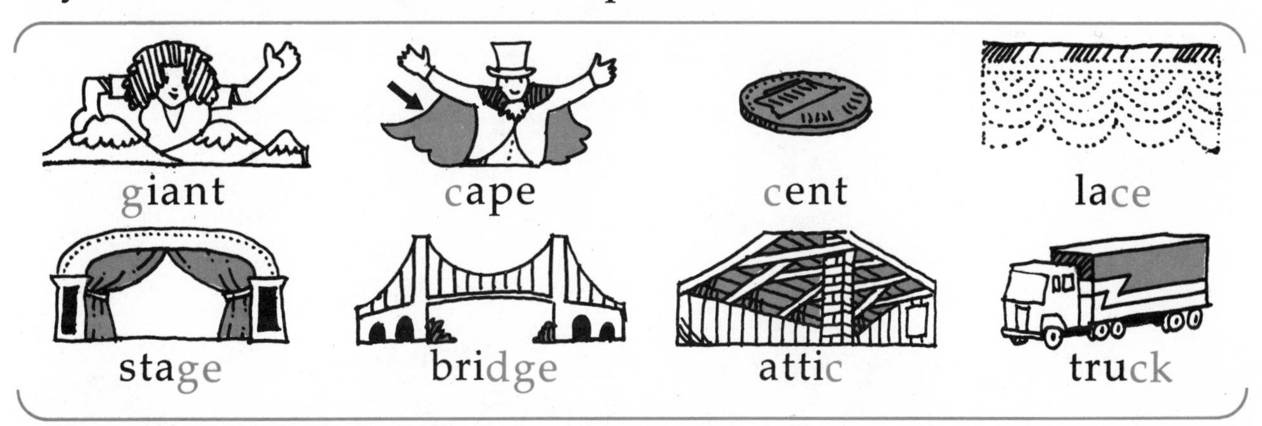

Say the word or words. Name the pictures in the row. Put an X on each picture with a name that has the same sound as the underlined letter or letters.

1. giant
2. cape
3. certain
   lace
4. stage
   bridge
5. attic
   truck

USING WHAT YOU KNOW

George put on his black cape and top hat. Then he walked to the center of the stage. His friends were sitting around the stage.

George pulled off his hat. "I will do a magic trick," he said. "I will have a tiger come out of this hat."

Look at the letters in color. Knowing the sounds the letters stand for helps you read the words.

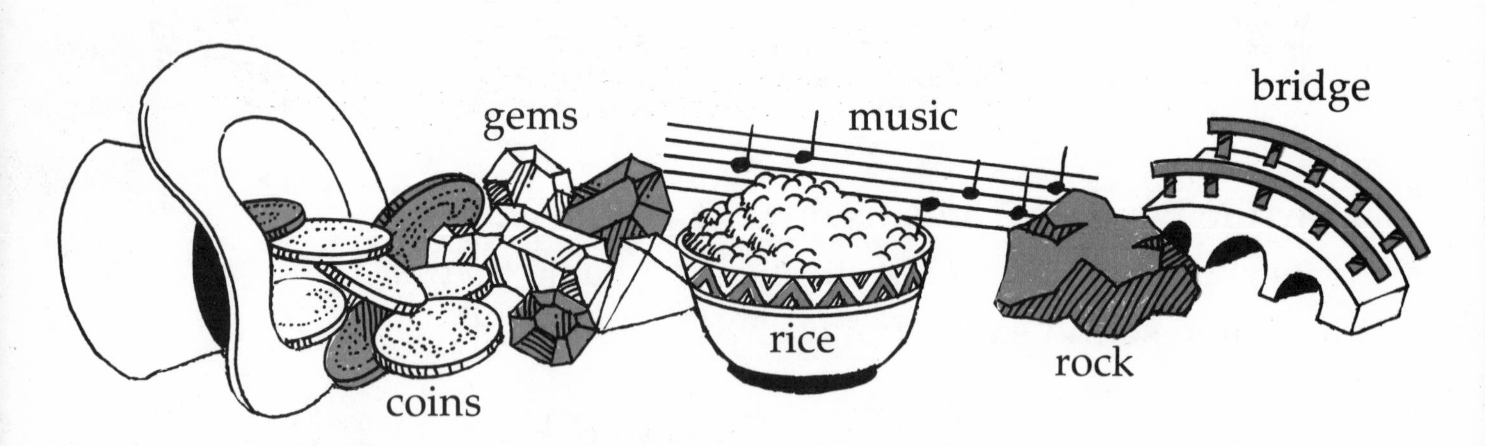

Look at the things coming out of the magic hat. Find the word for each thing in the puzzle. Look across and down. Circle each word.

m	b	r	i	d	g	e
u	y	i	h	f	e	r
s	l	c	r	q	m	o
i	p	e	j	g	s	c
c	o	i	n	s	x	k

 Consonant sound-letter correspondences: initial /j/ *g*, /k/ *c*, /s/ *c*; final /j/ *dge*, *ge*, /k/ *c*, *ck*, /s/ *ce*; using consonant sounds to decode words

WHILE YOU READ

Tip Use what you know about the sounds for letters to help you read new words.

George tapped the edge of his hat with his magic stick. Two gentle mice in a cage came out.

"That is not a tiger," said Cindy.

"I will try again," said George. He tapped his stick three times. He turned over the hat. A 50 cent piece fell out.

"That is a nice trick," said Cindy. "But that is not a tiger."

"Let me try once more," said George.

He tapped his stick again. A striped kitten jumped out of the hat. It was the colors of a tiger.

"It is a baby tiger!" said George.

AFTER YOU READ

A. Fill in the circle for the answer.

1. What came out of the hat first?

○ a baby ○ two mice ○ a tiger

2. The last thing that came out of the hat was

○ a kitten ○ 50 cents ○ a stick

3. How do you think Cindy felt at the end?

○ unhappy ○ important ○ surprised

B. Pretend you are doing magic tricks. Draw pictures to show what comes out of a magic hat.

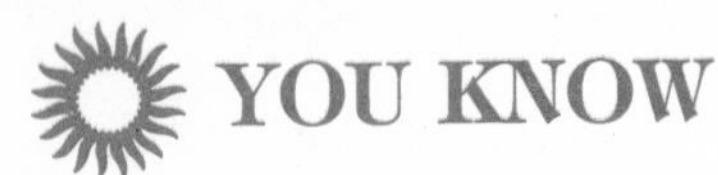

- Letters stand for sounds.
- Some letters stand for more than one sound.
- Different letters can stand for the same sound.

1. Name the picture. Circle the letter that stands for the sound at the beginning of the picture name.

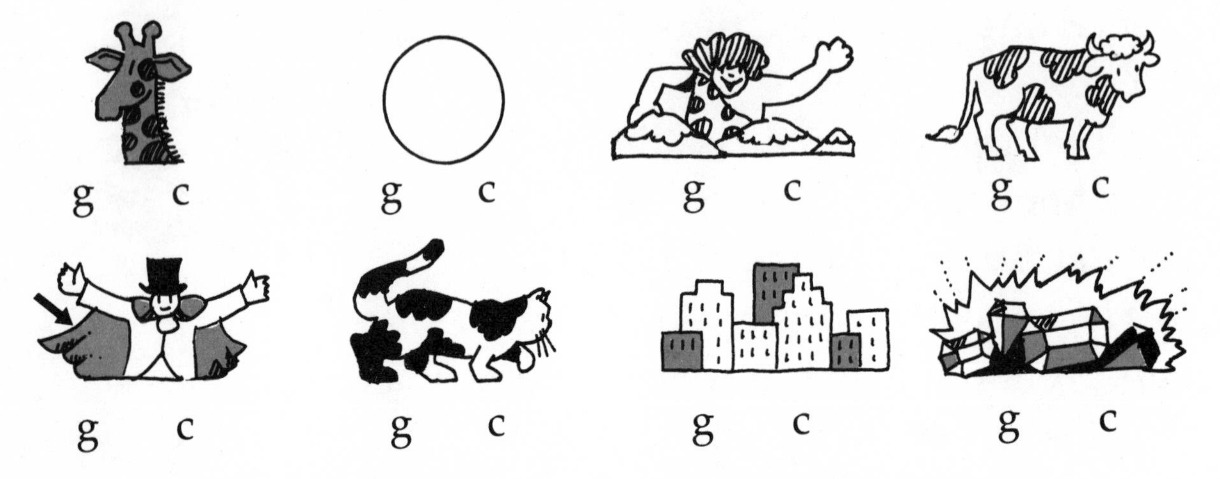

2. Name the picture. Circle the letter or letters that stand for the sound at the end of the picture name.

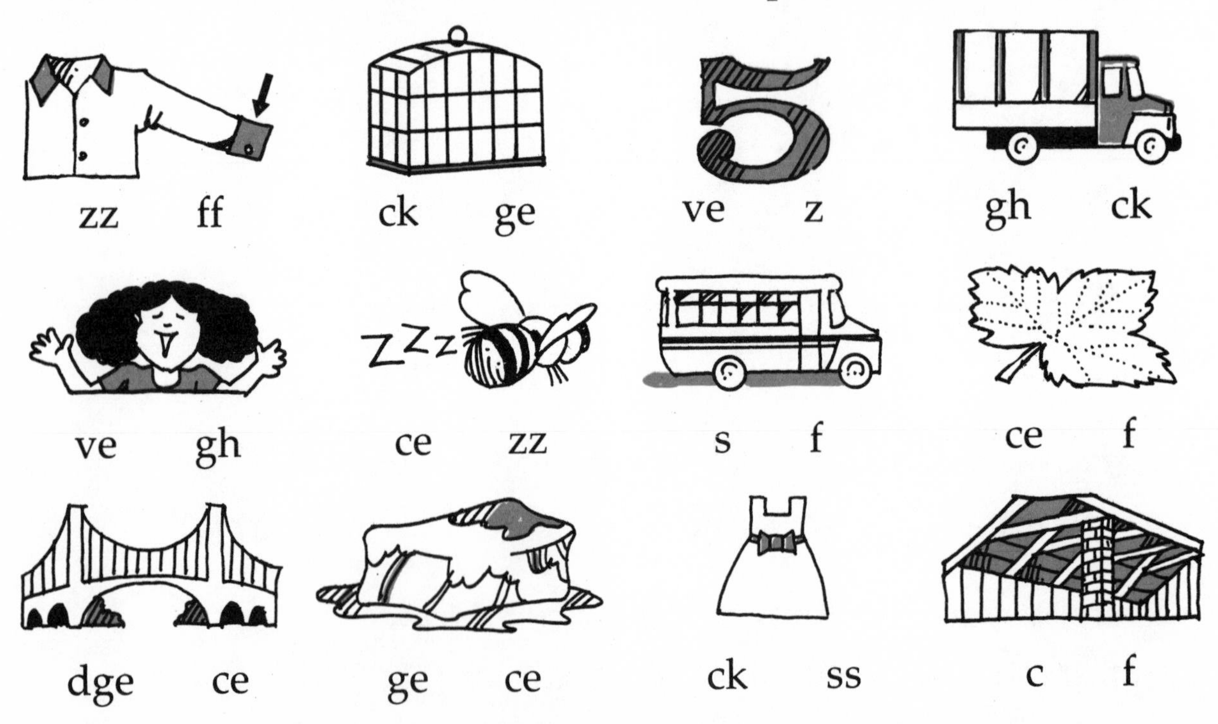

USING WHAT YOU KNOW

A giant truck was going to the city. A car and a school bus drove along behind it.

The road went under a bridge. The huge truck tried to go under the bridge, too. But there was not enough room. The truck was too large. Its roof hit the bottom of the bridge. The truck got stuck.

The car could pass the truck. The school bus could not pass. The bus was stuck, too.

A. Read the words. Find words in the story that rhyme. Write the words.

1. rough ______________

2. proof ______________

3. grass ______________

4. luck ______________ ______________

B. Read the words. Find words in the story that begin with the same sound. Write the words.

1. cent ______________

2. gems ______________

3. can ______________ ______________

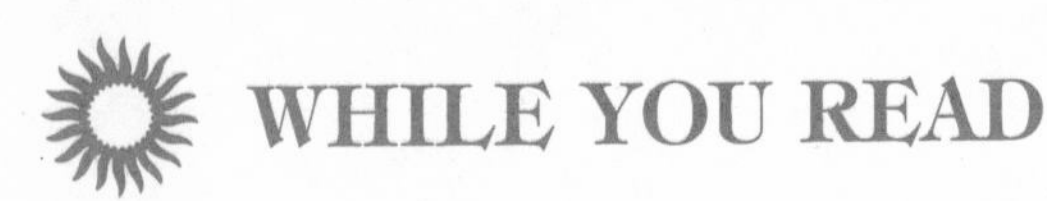

WHILE YOU READ

Use what you know about the sounds for letters to help you read new words.

The bus driver got off the bus. She went to look at the stuck truck.

"This is bad luck," said the truck driver. "My boss will be cross."

"I have an idea," the bus driver said. She pointed to the roof of the truck. "The truck will go down if you can let some air out of the tires. Then the truck may move.

The truck driver did what the bus driver said. Her idea worked. The truck driver gave a wave. Then they both drove off.

AFTER YOU READ

A. Fill in the circle for the answer.

1. The truck could move at last because

○ the driver looked at the roof

○ the driver let air out of the tires

○ the boss had some good luck

2. The story was mostly about a

○ cross boss ○ flat tire ○ stuck truck

3. The bus driver in the story was

○ smart ○ mean ○ happy

B. Draw or find pictures of different kinds of trucks. Cut them out. Paste them on paper. Write a sentence about each truck.

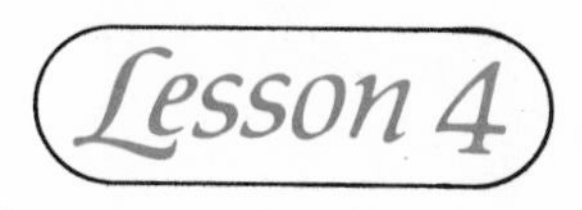

CONSONANT BLENDS / READING WORDS IN CONTEXT

- Sometimes letters like fl or br come together at the beginning of a word.
- The sounds two letters stand for together can seem to be almost one sound.

Say the word that names each picture.

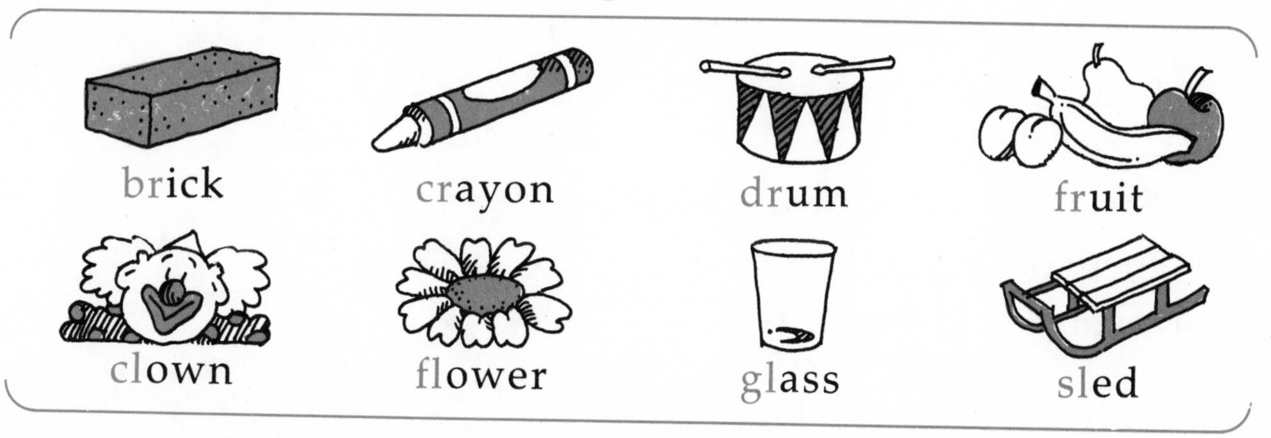

Name the picture. Draw a line under the letters that stand for the sounds you hear at the beginning of the picture name.

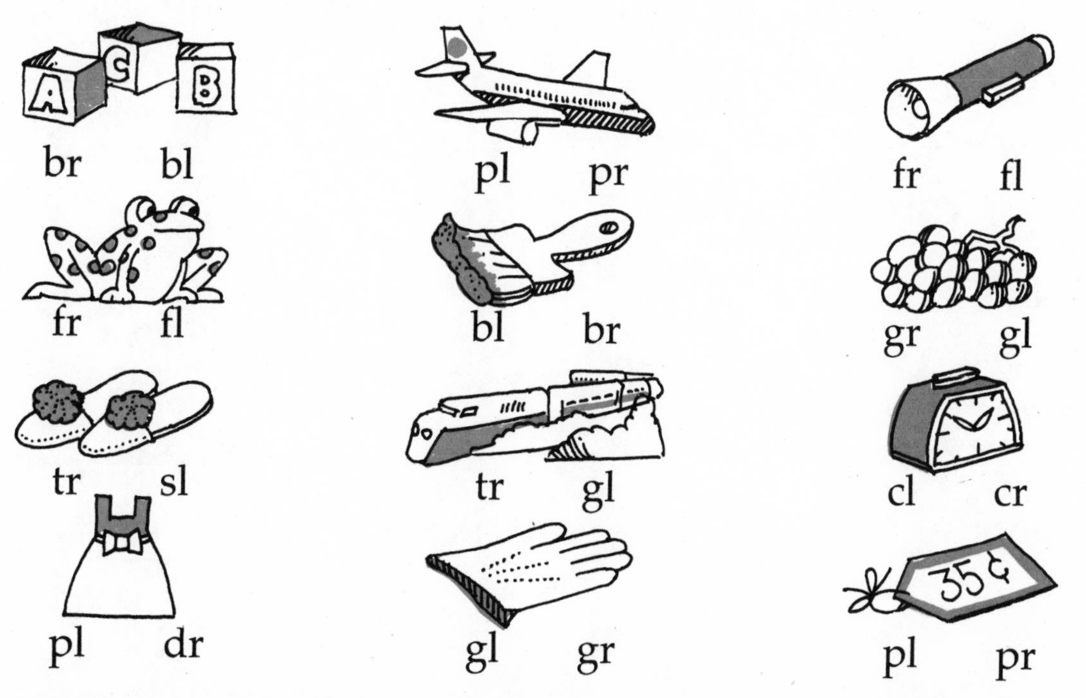

USING WHAT YOU KNOW

Brad and Trish were playing in the park. Trish found a black box in the grass. The box had two buttons in front. One button was green. The other button was clear.

"What do you think will happen if I press a button?" Trish asked.

"Do not try it!" cried Brad. But it was too late. Trish had already pressed the green button.

Say the sounds for the letters in color together so they are almost one sound. This helps you read the words.

Here are some things Brad and Trish saw in the park. Read word 1. Find 1 in the puzzle. Write the word after 1 in the puzzle. Put one letter in each box. Do the same thing for the other words.

1. trees
2. clouds
3. slide
4. frog
5. grass
6. ground

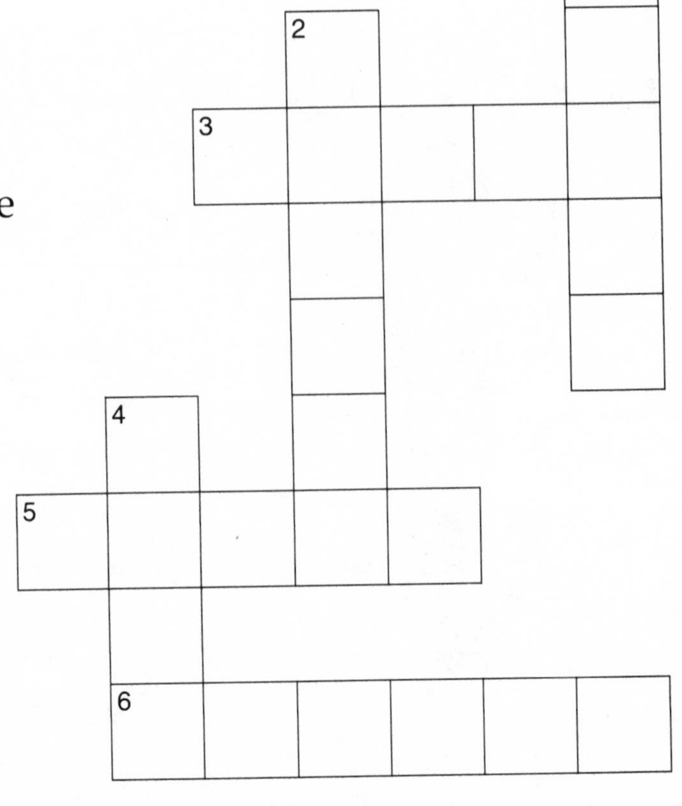

 Consonant blend sound-letter correspondences: initial *l* and *r* blends; using consonant sounds to decode words

WHILE YOU READ

Look for letters like gl, sl, cl, or tr at the beginning of a word. Say the sounds for the letters together as you read the word.

Each time Trish pressed the green button, green light came from the box. The thing the light hit slowly turned green. Trish made a blue bird turn green. She made a brown tree trunk turn green. She made a black fly turn green.

Trish turned to Brad. She pressed the green button. Brad turned green.

"I do not want to be green!" Brad cried.

"Maybe I should try the clear button," said Trish. She pressed the clear button. Brad turned his own color. Brad was glad he was no longer green.

AFTER YOU READ

A. Fill in the circle for the answer.

1. The light from the box made things

○ grow ○ green ○ black

2. The first thing that turned green was

○ Brad ○ a bird ○ a tree

3. The clear button makes everything turn

○ its own color ○ brown ○ black and blue

B. Get a crayon for each color named in the story. Draw a picture to go with the story.

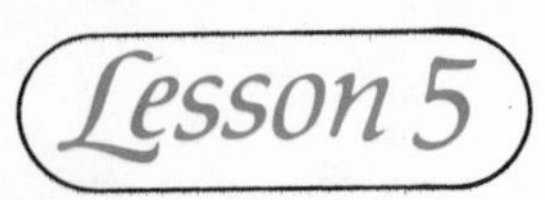

CONSONANT BLENDS / READING WORDS IN CONTEXT

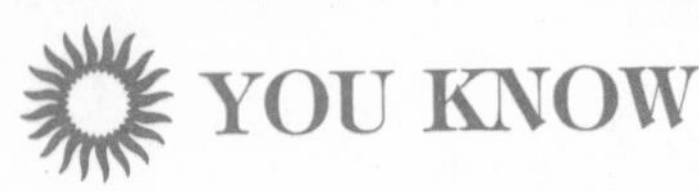

- Sometimes letters like nt and sk come together at the end of a word.
- The sounds two letters stand for together can seem to be almost one sound.

Say the word that names each picture.

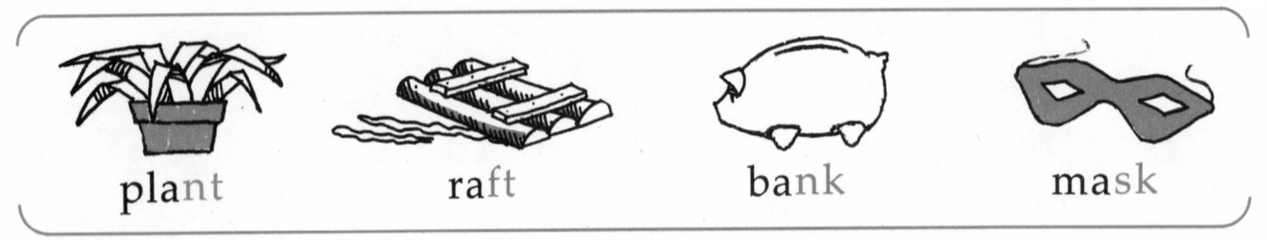

Name the picture. Draw a line to the letters that stand for the sounds you hear at the end of the picture name.

 Consonant blend sound-letter correspondences: final /ft/ *ft*, /ld/ *ld*, /lt/ *lt*, /mp/ *mp*, /nd/ *nd*, /ngk/ *nk*, /nt/ *nt*, /sk/ *sk*, /st/ *st*; using consonant sounds to decode words

USING WHAT YOU KNOW

Dear Hank,

Can you come to Camp Wind with me? We will sleep in a tent. We will swim in a pond. We may see some wild animals. Ask your mom and dad. This will be the best week you will ever spend.

Your friend,
Harold

Say the sounds for the letters in color together so they are almost one sound. This helps you read the words.

A. Write the word that goes in the sentence.

1. Pond water can be ______________.
   cold wild

2. You use a tent on ______________.
   wind land

3. You can ______________ into a pond.
   jump lift

4. Harold puts a ______________ on the letter.
   plant stamp

B. Find 1 in the puzzle. Look at the word you wrote in sentence 1. Write the word after 1 in the puzzle. Put one letter on each line. Do the same thing for the other words.

1. ___ ___ ___ ___

2. ___ ___ ___ ___

3. ___ ___ ___ ___

4. ___ ___ ___ ___ ___

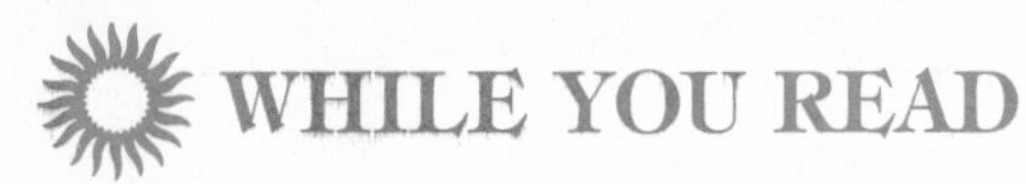

WHILE YOU READ

Look for letters like ft, mp, nk, or st at the end of a word. Say the sounds for the letters together as you read the word.

Harold and Hank were in their tent. They heard something go bump. It made them jump.

"What do you think is out there?" asked Hank. "I hope it is not a ghost!"

"You look," said Harold. "Lift the tent flap."

"But what if I find a wild beast?" Hank asked. He felt cold all over.

Hank peeked out. The moon was bright. He looked around. Something was on a tree stump. "Yikes!" he whispered. He quickly shut the tent flap. "It is not a ghost. It is a skunk!"

AFTER YOU READ

A. Fill in the circle for the answer.

1. The story took place in the

○ night ○ afternoon ○ morning

2. When Hank peeked out of the tent, he was

○ happy ○ hungry ○ scared

3. What do you think the boys will do?

○ shout at the skunk ○ stay in the tent ○ run away

B. Some camping words are woods, snake, grass, lake, and hike. Use these words or your own. Write three sentences about a day at a camp.

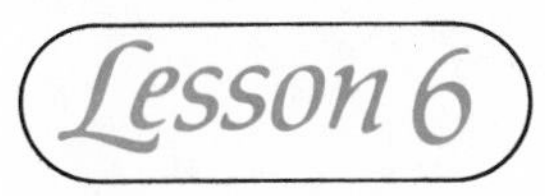

CONSONANT DIGRAPHS / READING WORDS IN CONTEXT

YOU KNOW

- Sometimes the letters ch, sh, th, or wh come together at the beginning of a word.
- Sometimes the letters ch, ng, sh, tch, or th come together at the end of a word.
- Two letters together can stand for one sound.

Say the word that names each picture.

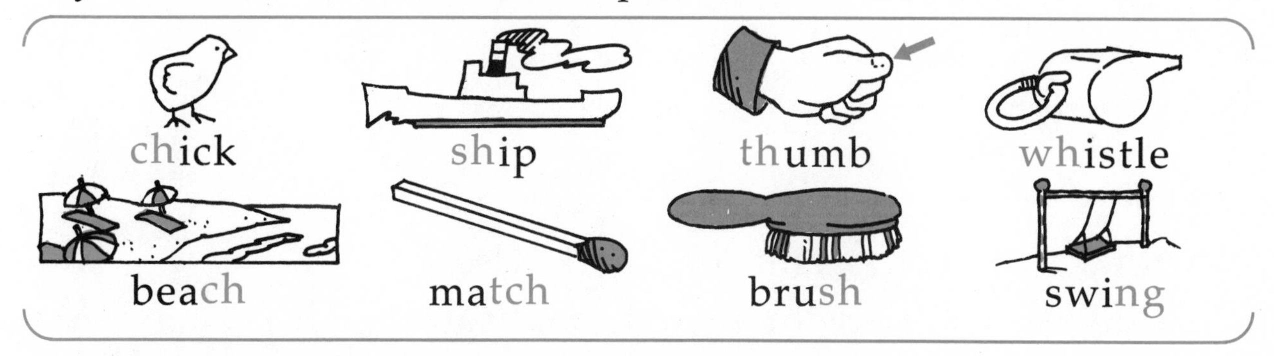

1. Name the picture. Draw a line under the letters that stand for the sound you hear at the beginning of the picture name.

sh wh

th sh

ch th

wh sh

2. Name the picture. Draw a line to the letters that stand for the sound you hear at the end of the picture name.

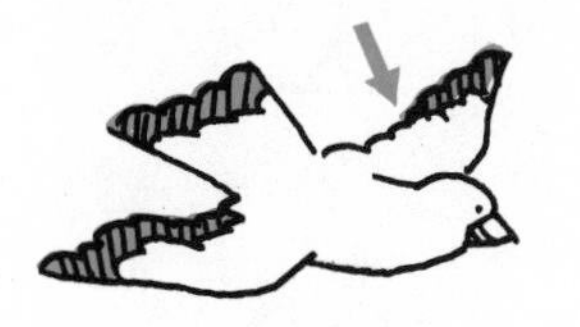

ch
ng

sh
ch

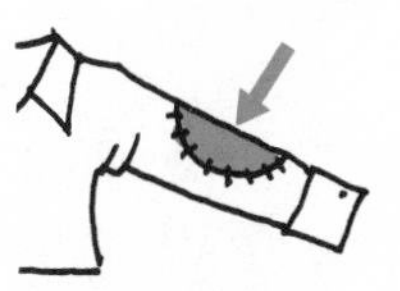

th
tch

th
ch

sh
ch

ng
sh

USING WHAT YOU KNOW

Both a shark and a whale live in water. A shark is a fish. A whale is not a fish. A fish can stay under water all the time. A whale must reach into the air to take a breath.

A whale can do one thing most animals cannot do. A whale can sing.

Say the words with letters in color. Listen for the sound the letters stand for. The two letters together stand for one sound.

1. Color the picture. Use green for each part with a word that begins like shark. Use gray for each part with a word that begins like where. Use brown for each part with a word that begins like child. Use blue for each part with a word that ends like sing.

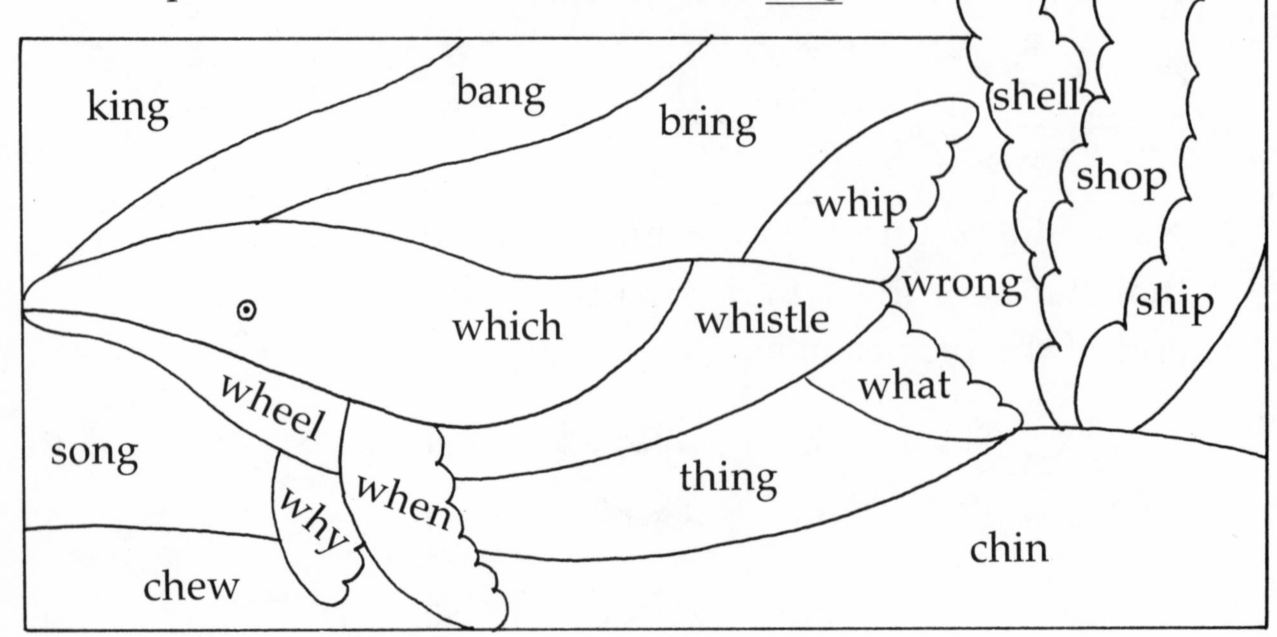

2. This is not a fish. It is a picture of a ______________.

 Consonant digraph sound-letter correspondences: initial /ch/ *ch*, /sh/ *sh*, /th/ *th*, /hw/ *wh*; final /ch/ *ch*, *tch*, /ng/ *ng*, /sh/ *sh*, /th/ *th*; using consonant sounds to decode words

WHILE YOU READ

Look for letters like ch, sh, th, or wh at the beginning or end of a word. Say the word so the letters together stand for one sound.

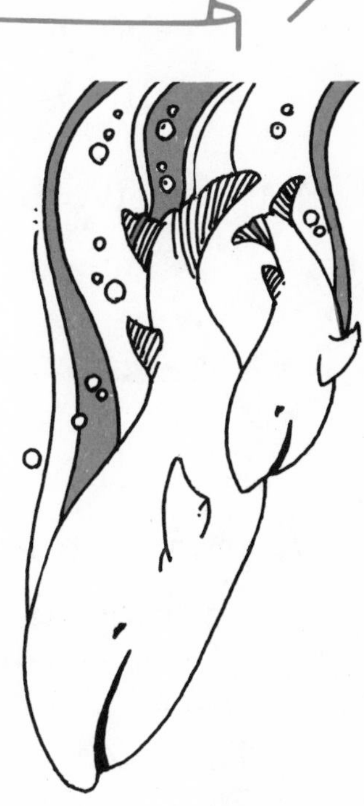

A whale is born in water. It lives in water all its life. But it cannot take a breath in water. It must have air.

A mother whale can teach her baby what it needs to know. She can teach it to dive deep. She can teach it to hold its breath in water. A mother whale also keeps her baby safe. She chases away sharks that may hurt it.

A father whale can help keep a baby whale from getting lost. The father whale sings. The baby whale listens for the song of its father. Then it knows where to swim to find its family.

AFTER YOU READ

A. Fill in the circle for the answer.

1. A baby whale does not get lost because

○ it can hold its breath

○ it hears the song of its father

○ its mother can teach it how to swim

2. What is the story mostly about?

○ whale songs ○ baby whales ○ mother sharks

B. Pretend you are in a ship that can go under water. Draw a picture of what you see.

Lesson 7 SILENT CONSONANTS / READING WORDS IN CONTEXT

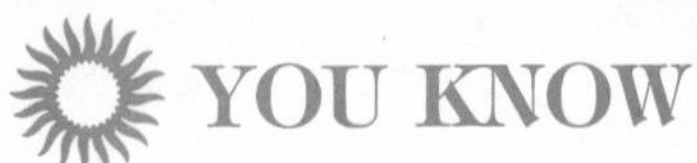

YOU KNOW

- Sometimes the letters kn or wr come together at the beginning of a word.
- Sometimes a letter in a word is not part of the sound of the word.

Say the word that names each picture.

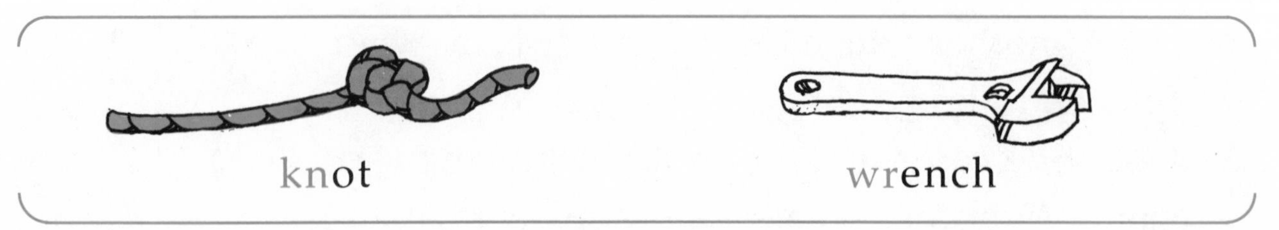

A. Name the picture. Circle the word that names the picture.

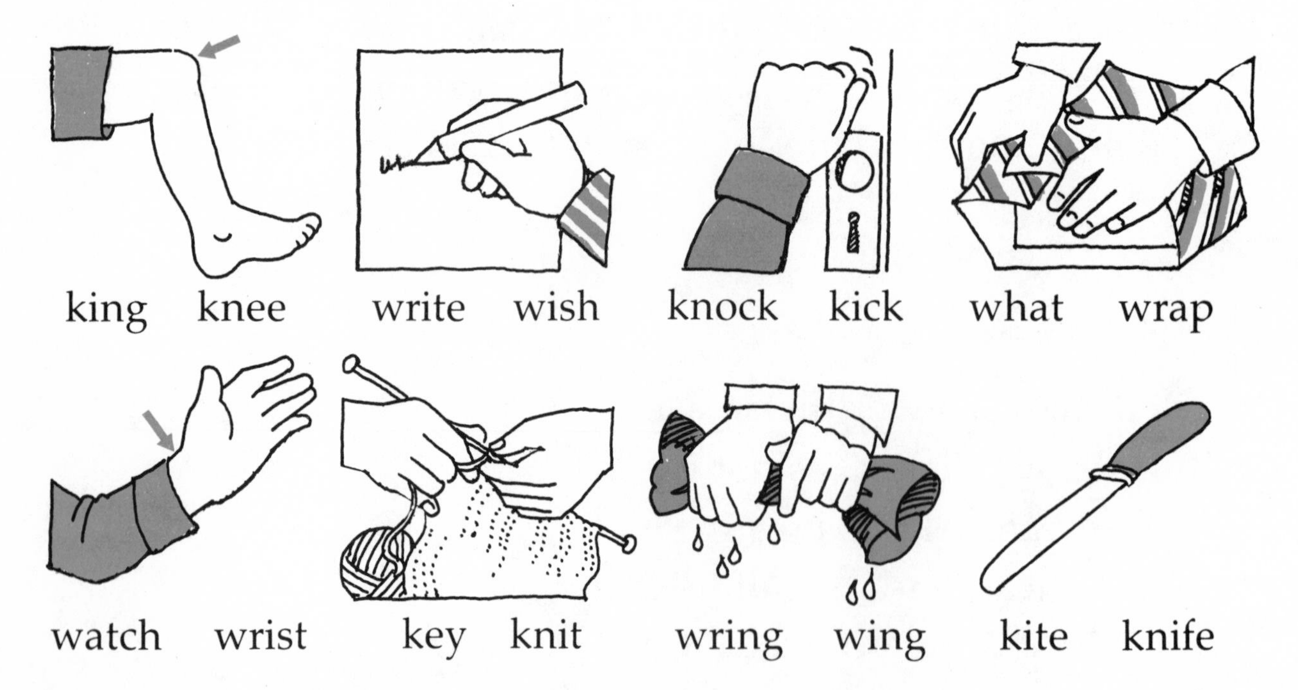

B. 1. Circle the letter that stands for the sound you hear at the beginning of the word knot. k n t

2. Circle the letter that stands for the sound you hear at the beginning of the word wrench. w n r

 Consonant sound-letter correspondences: /n/ *kn*, /r/ *wr*; using consonant sounds to decode words

USING WHAT YOU KNOW

You have two legs. Each leg has a knee, so you have two knees. Do you know how many knees animals have? Most animals have four legs. Do they have four knees, too? If you think they do, you are wrong. An elephant is the only animal that has four knees.

Look at the letters in color. When you see the letters kn or wr at the beginning of a word, say the word so you begin with the sound for the second letter.

Read clue 1. Find the answer in the box. Write the answer next to 1 in the puzzle. Put one letter in each box. Do the same thing for the other clues.

write	knock	wrong	knees	knife	knot

1. You can tie a rope into a ______.
2. You do this on a door.
3. You need a pencil to do this.
4. An elephant has four of these.
5. Something that is not right is ______.
6. You use this to cut your food.

1.	☐	☐	☐	☐			
2.	☐	☐	☐	☐	☐		
	3.	☐	☐	☐	☐	☐	
	4.	☐	☐	☐	☐	☐	
		5.	☐	☐	☐	☐	☐
		6.	☐	☐	☐	☐	☐

WHILE YOU READ

Tip: Look for the letters kn or wr at the beginning of a word. Say the word so you begin with the sound for the second letter.

EVA: I am like an elephant. I never forget.
JANE: If I went away for two years, would you know me?
EVA: Yes.
JANE: If I went away for ten years, would you know me?
EVA: Yes.
JANE: Would you know me after 20 years?
EVA: Yes.
JANE: Knock, knock.
EVA: Who is there?
JANE: See, you were wrong. You forgot me already!

AFTER YOU READ

A. Fill in the circle for the answer.

1. Eva asked, "Who is there?" because
- ○ she forgot Jane
- ○ Jane said, "Knock, knock"
- ○ Jane went away for two years

2. This story is
○ sad ○ wrong ○ silly

B. Read the story out loud with a friend. Take turns reading what Eva and Jane say.

YOU KNOW

- Sometimes letters like ch, kn, pl, or tr come together at the beginning of a word.
- Sometimes letters like nk, st, or th come together at the end of a word.

1. Name the picture. Draw a line under the letters that stand for the sound or sounds you hear at the beginning of the picture name.

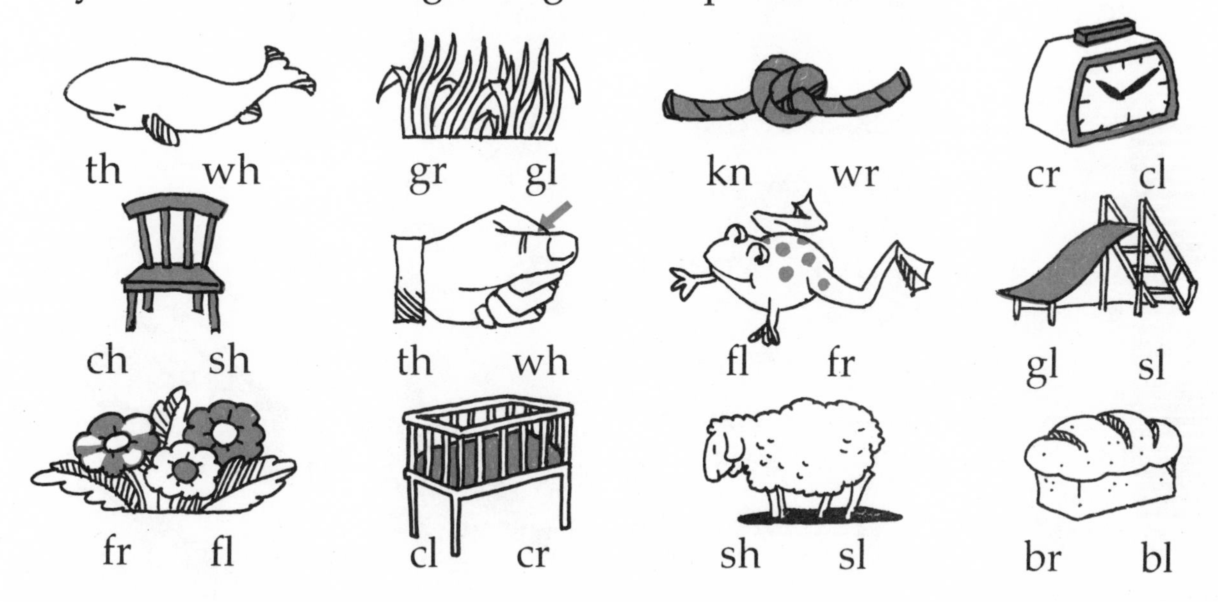

2. Name the picture. Draw a line under the letters that stand for the sound or sounds you hear at the end of the picture name.

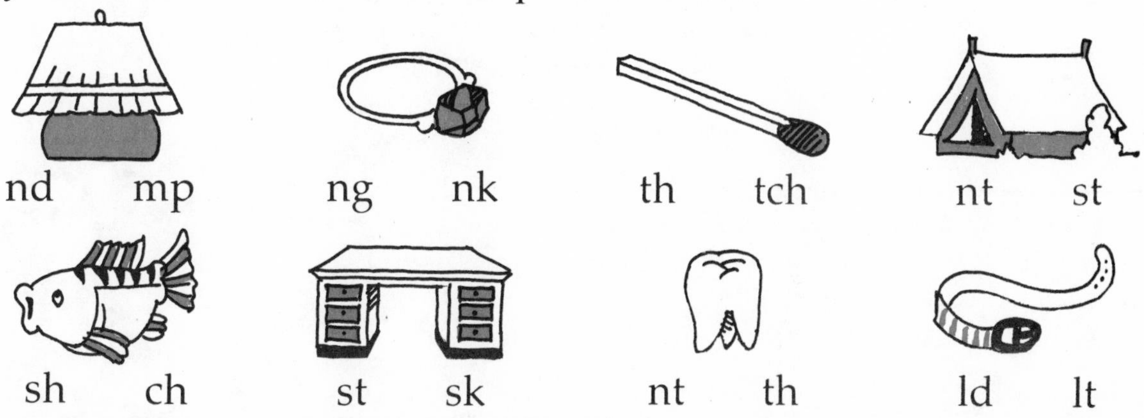

USING WHAT YOU KNOW

It was a pretty day. White clouds sailed across the blue sky. Birds sang. A squirrel jumped from tree to tree. An old frog sat near a pond. It had just shed its skin. Its new green skin was smooth and shiny. The frog seemed to be sleeping.

A crow sat on a branch of a tree. It saw the old frog. The crow thought the frog would make a good lunch.

Read the words. Look at the picture. Write the word that names each part of the picture.

frog branch crow pond sky tree bird cloud

____

____

____

____

____

____

____

____

 Review—consonant blend, consonant digraph, and consonant sound-letter correspondences: initial, final; using consonant sounds to decode words

WHILE YOU READ

Tip Look for letters like dr, fl, ld, ng, th, or wr at the beginning or end of a word. Use what you know about the sound or sounds for the letters to help you read the word.

The crow flew down quietly. It stepped along slowly. It drew closer to the frog. Then it opened its mouth and snapped at the frog.

Splash! The old frog jumped into the pond. It had not been asleep after all. Quick as a flash, it swam away in the cold water.

The crow thought it would catch the frog. It was wrong. Now the crow would have to find another lunch. That old frog fooled the crow.

AFTER YOU READ

A. Fill in the circle for the answer.

1. Where did the frog jump?

○ over the crow ○ on the lunch ○ into the pond

2. The frog fooled the crow because it

○ knew the crow was coming
○ liked to swim
○ was asleep

3. From the story, you know the crow was

○ hungry ○ scared ○ sleepy

B. What do you think the crow did next? Draw a picture.

YOU KNOW

- The letters a, e, i, o, and u can stand for short vowel sounds.
- Sometimes the letters aw, ea, or oo come together in a word.

Say the word that names each picture. Each word has a short vowel sound.

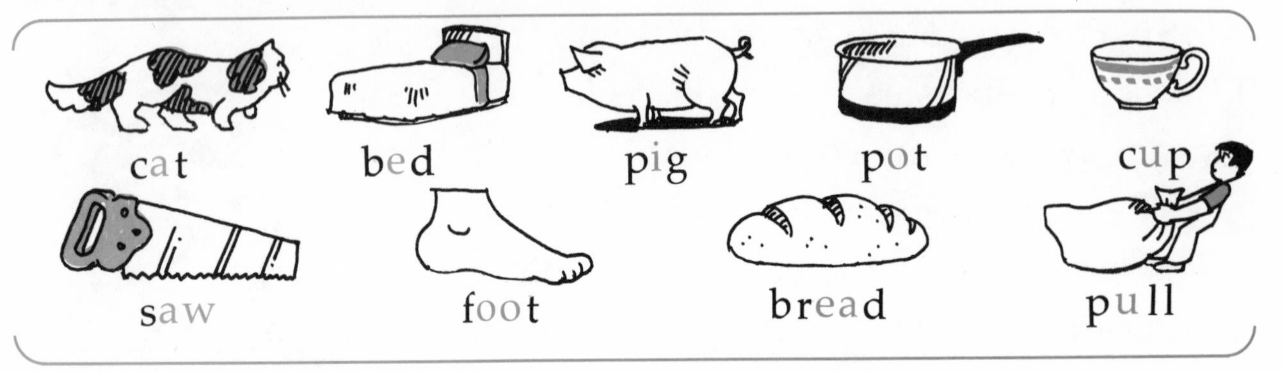

Name the picture. Circle the letter or letters that stand for the vowel sound in the picture name.

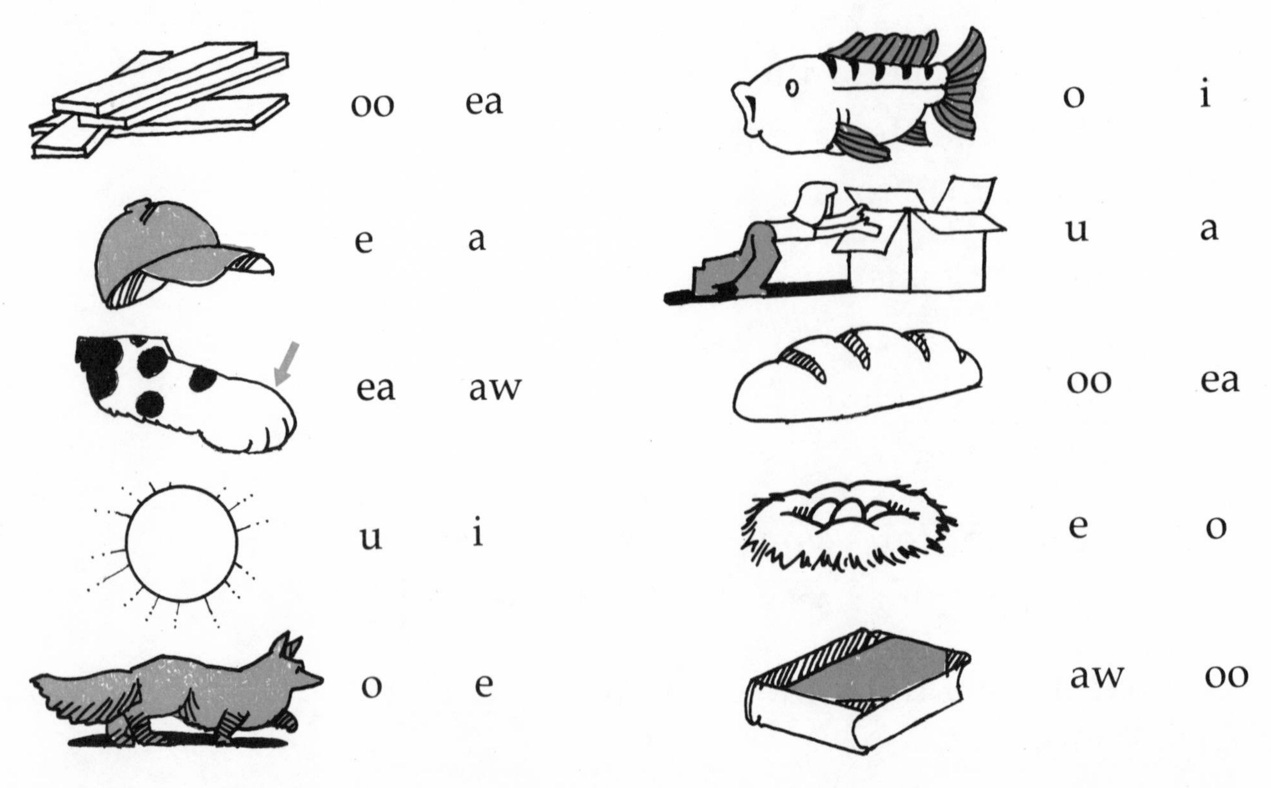

 Short vowel sound-letter correspondences: /a/ *a*, /e/ *e*, *ea*, /i/ *i*, /o/ *o*, /ô/ *aw*, /u/ *u*, /ů/ *oo*, *u*; using vowel sounds to decode words

USING WHAT YOU KNOW

Animals live in the woods. How can an animal protect itself from an enemy? An animal can pull down its head and run. An animal can put up a fight. Or an animal can trick its enemy.

A fawn is a little deer. It has spots. The spots help the fawn hide in the woods. Hiding protects the fawn from its enemy.

Look at the letters in color. Knowing the short vowel sounds the letters stand for helps you read the words.

Name the animals in the picture. Then write each animal name under the letter or letters that stand for the vowel sound you hear in the animal name.

a

____

aw

____

i

____

o

____

____

u

____

____

Short vowel sound-letter correspondences: /a/ *a*, /e/ *e*, *ea*, /i/ *i*, /o/ *o*, /ô/ *aw*, /u/ *u*, /ù/ *oo*, *u*; using vowel sounds to decode words

WHILE YOU READ

Look for a, e, i, o, or u in a word. Also look for aw, ea, or oo together in a word. Use what you know about the short vowel sound for the letter or letters to help you read the word.

Some animals run from an enemy. A rabbit runs away. A frog jumps into the water and swims off.

A bear fights an enemy. It hits with its legs. It pushes and pulls with its claws. A wolf fights, too. It grabs things in its jaws.

A possum tricks an enemy. It lies down and is very still. It looks dead, so its enemy runs off. Then the possum gets up. It is not dead after all.

AFTER YOU READ

A. Fill in the circle for the answer.

1. Which animal fights an enemy?

○ a goat ○ a possum ○ a wolf

2. An enemy of a possum runs off because the possum

○ bites it ○ looks dead ○ pushes it

3. The story is mostly about ways animals

○ stay safe ○ play tricks ○ fight bears

B. Pick one of the animals in the story. Draw a picture of it staying safe from an enemy.

 Short vowel sound-letter correspondences: /a/ *a*, /e/ *e*, *ea*, /i/ *i*, /o/ *o*, /ô/ *aw*, /u/ *u*, /ù/ *oo*, *u*; using vowel sounds to decode words

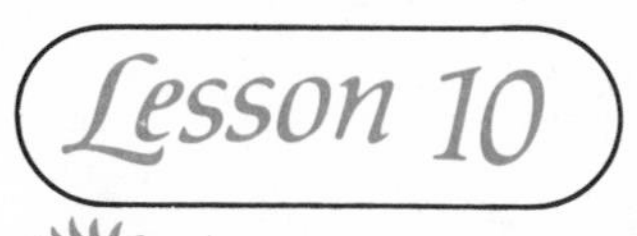

VOWELS / READING WORDS IN CONTEXT

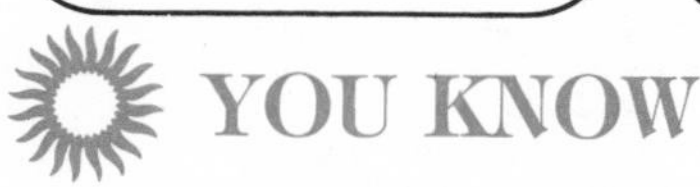

- The vowel letters and y can stand for long vowel sounds.
- Sometimes letters like ai, ie, oa, and ue come together in a word.

Say the word that names each picture. Each word has a long vowel sound.

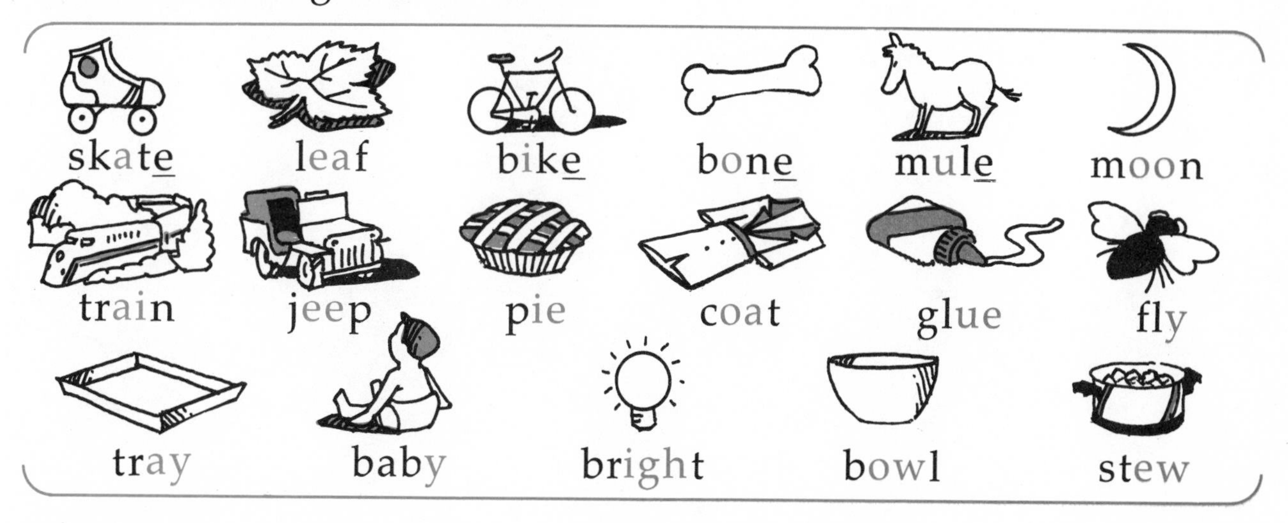

Name each picture. Draw a line to the letter or letters that stand for the vowel sound you hear in the picture name.

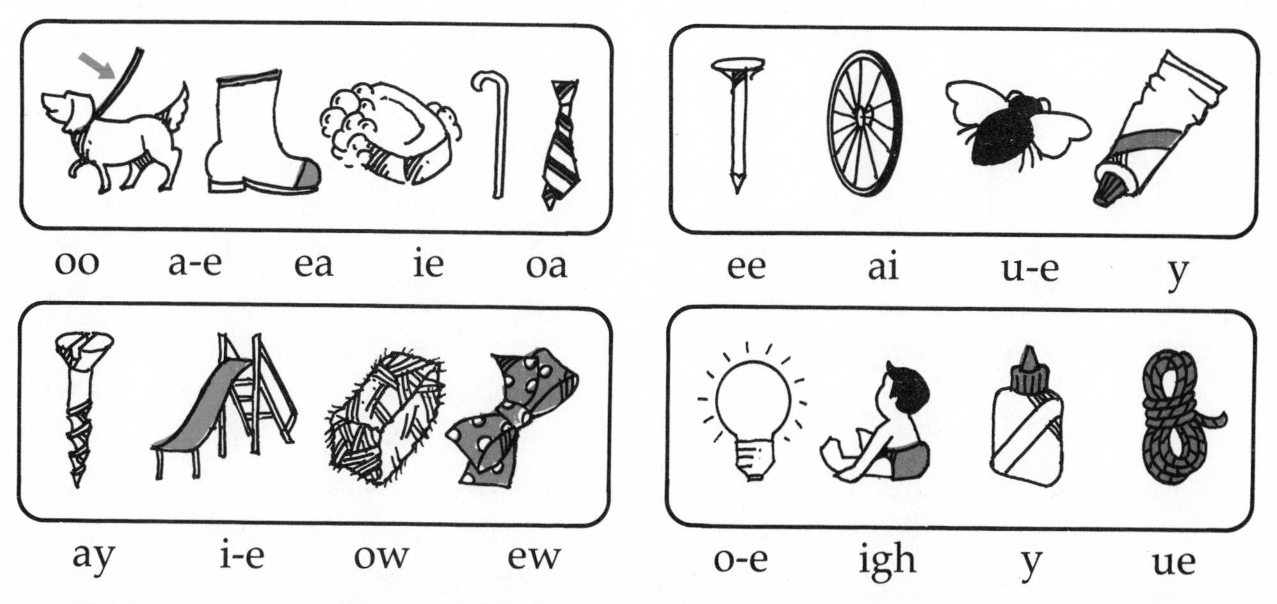

Long vowel sound-letter correspondences: /ā/ *a-e, ai, ay,* /ē/ *ea, ee, y,* /ī/ *i-e, ie, igh, y,* /ō/ *o-e, oa, ow,* /o͞o/ *u-e, ew, oo, ue;* using vowel sounds to decode words

USING WHAT YOU KNOW

The children are at a party for Sue. They play a nice new game. Lew takes a tail. He wants to put it on the mule. He cannot see, but he will try to reach the mule. Is his hand too high? Is his hand too low? Lew hopes he will put the tail in the right place.

Look at the letters in color. Knowing the long vowel sounds the letters stand for helps you read the words.

A. Write the word that goes in the sentence.

1. Lew put a ____________ on the mule.
chew tail

2. Did he get it in the ____________ place?
right peek

3. Maybe he put it on the ____________.
sky dream

4. Or did he stick it on the ____________?
lie road

5. No, Lew put a tail on the ____________!
true moon

B. Look at the words you wrote in part A. Circle each word in the puzzle. Look across and down.

m	a	r	o	a	d	t
o	u	a	i	l	y	a
o	r	i	g	h	t	i
n	a	s	k	y	w	l

 Long vowel sound-letter correspondences: /ā/ *a-e, ai, ay,* /ē/ *ea, ee, y,* /ī/ *i-e, ie, igh, y,* /ō/ *o-e, oa, ow,* /o͞o/ *u-e, ew, oo, ue;* using vowel sounds to decode words

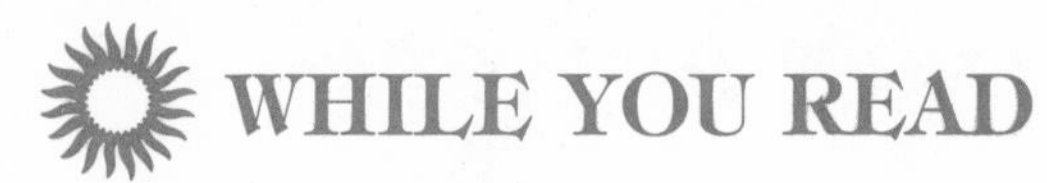

WHILE YOU READ

Tip Look for a, i, o, u, or y in a word. Also look for letters like ay, ee, or ew together in a word. Use what you know about the long vowel sound for the letter or letters to help you read the word.

Soon it is time for May to take a tail. She will try to place it on the mule.

May cannot see. She does not know which way to go. She does not have a clue. So May does not go to the right place. She does not even get close. She almost leaves the room!

May does not find the mule. She finds Sue. May puts the tail on the boat that Lew gave Sue!

AFTER YOU READ

A. Fill in the circle for the answer.

1. Where does May put the tail?

   ○ on Lew ○ on the room ○ on a boat

2. May does not find the mule because she

   ○ cannot see it ○ is too tall ○ is close to it

3. This story is about

   ○ a clue ○ May ○ Sue

B. Draw a big picture of an animal without a tail. Cut out a tail and put tape on it. Ask a friend to cover his or her eyes and try to put the tail in the right place.

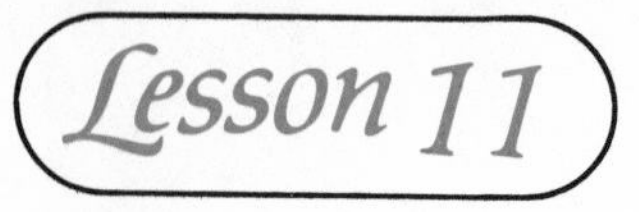

VOWELS / READING WORDS IN CONTEXT

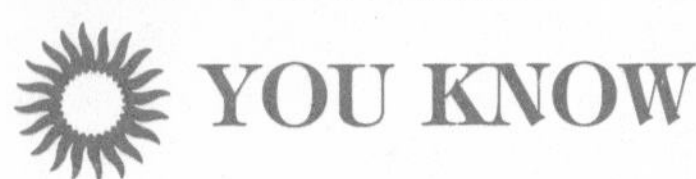

- Sometimes the letters oi, oy, ou, or ow come together in a word.
- Different letters can stand for the same sound.

Say the word that names each picture.

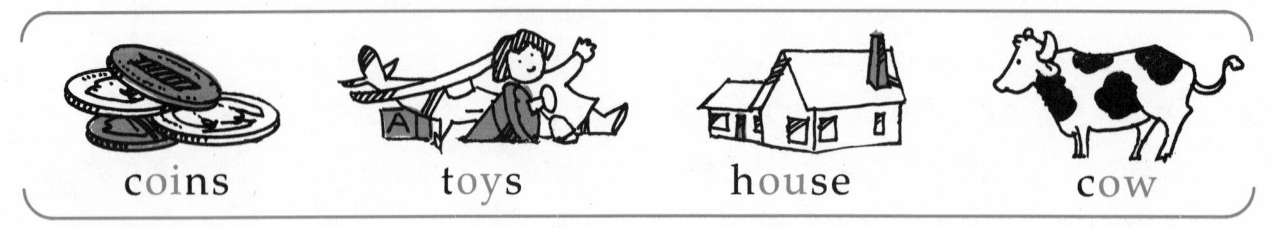

Name the picture. Circle the letters that stand for the vowel sound in the picture name.

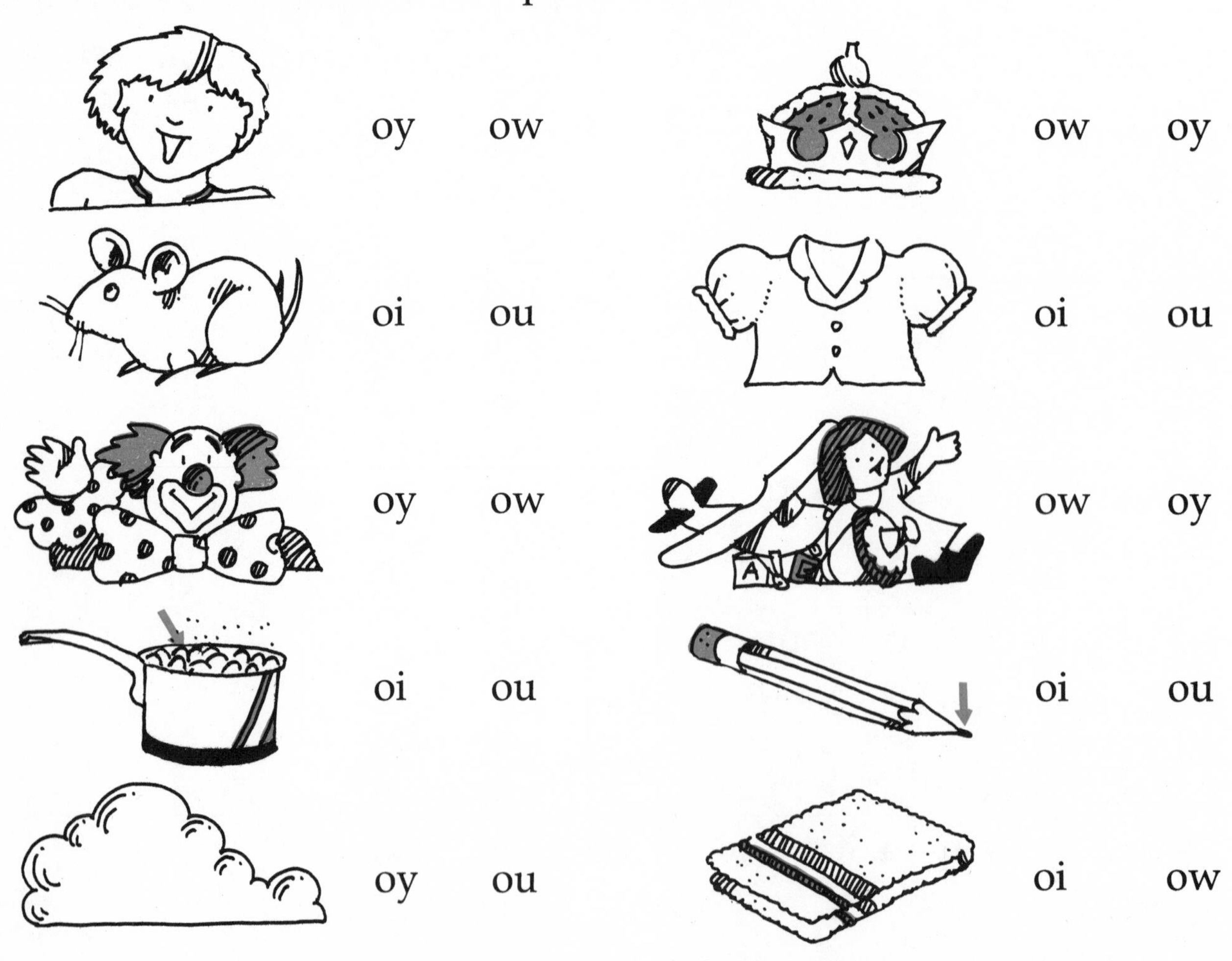

 Diphthong sound-letter correspondences: /oi/ *oi, oy,* /ou/ *ou, ow;* using vowel sounds to decode words

USING WHAT YOU KNOW

Look at the color letters in the words the girl said. The letters ow and ou stand for the same vowel sound. Look at the color letters in the words the boy said. The letters oy and oi stand for the same vowel sound.

Read the first word. Put a ✓ in front of the word that names something that might be found in the ground. The word must have the same vowel sound as the first word.

1. point	____ book	____ owl	____ coin
2. cow	____ mouse	____ town	____ coat
3. boy	____ noise	____ money	____ oil
4. ouch	____ cloud	____ crown	____ note
5. brown	____ clown	____ blouse	____ shoe
6. boil	____ clock	____ flower	____ toy
7. sound	____ towel	____ bone	____ house

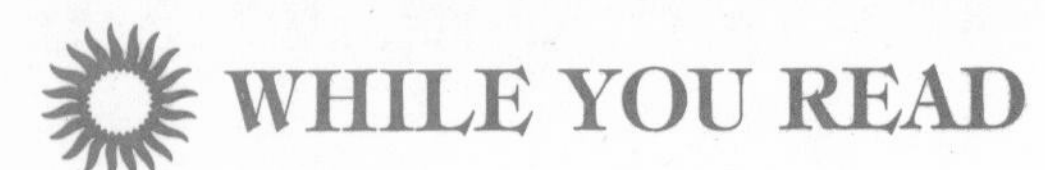

WHILE YOU READ

Look for the letters oi, oy, ou, or ow together in a word. Use what you know about the sound for the letters to help you read the word.

Joy dug around in the ground. She pulled out a round thing. It was covered with soil.

What had she found? It was not an old toy. It was not an old brown can. It was not an oil can. It was not a crown for a queen.

Howie cleaned off the soil from the round thing. Then he gave a loud shout. "Wow! Look at it now. See how it shines!" he said.

"Oh boy!" said Joy. "It is a gold coin. I wonder if there are any more in the ground."

AFTER YOU READ

A. Fill in the circle for the answer.

1. Joy found a

○ toy ○ coin ○ crown

2. What shape was the coin?

○ pointed ○ square ○ round

3. The coin was shiny because Howie

○ cleaned it ○ found it ○ covered it

4. At the end, Joy and Howie were

○ scared ○ tired ○ happy

B. Write what you think Joy and Howie will do next. Use words like found, coin, and ground.

Lesson 12 VOWELS / READING WORDS IN CONTEXT

YOU KNOW

- Sometimes the letters ar, er, ir, or, or ur come together in a word.

Say a word that names each picture. Each word has a vowel + r sound.

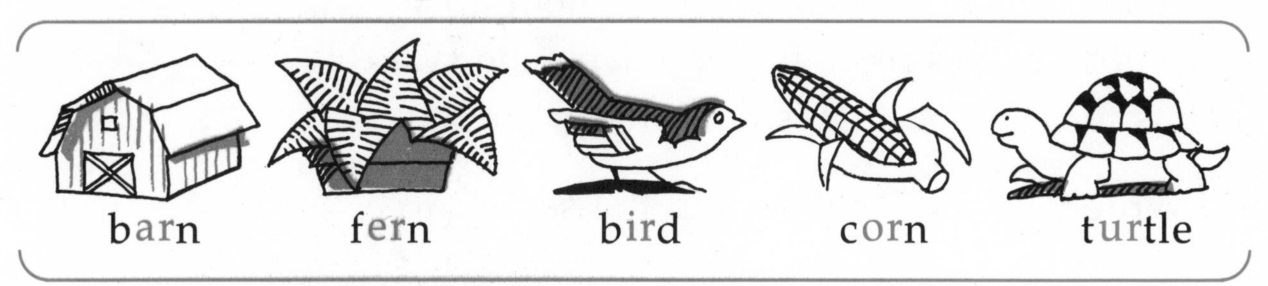

Name the picture. Draw a line under the letters that stand for the vowel + r sound you hear in the picture name.

r-controlled vowel sound-letter correspondences: /är/ *ar*, /ėr/ *er, ir, ur*, /ôr/ *or;* using vowel sounds to decode words

USING WHAT YOU KNOW

Do you like to eat corn? The part of the corn that you eat is the seeds. Corn seeds will turn into plants if you put them in dirt. But do not cook the seeds first.

Look at the letters in color. Sometimes when the letter r comes right after a vowel, the vowel stands for a sound that is not long or short.

A. Write the word that goes in the sentence.

1. Corn is grown on a ________________.
germ   farm

2. Some corn farms are very ________________.
large   purple

3. Corn plants grow in ________________.
barns   dirt

4. A person who grows corn is a ________________.
sport   farmer

B. Find 1 in the puzzle. Look at the word you wrote in sentence 1. Write the word after 1 in the puzzle. Put one letter on each line. Do the same thing for the other words.

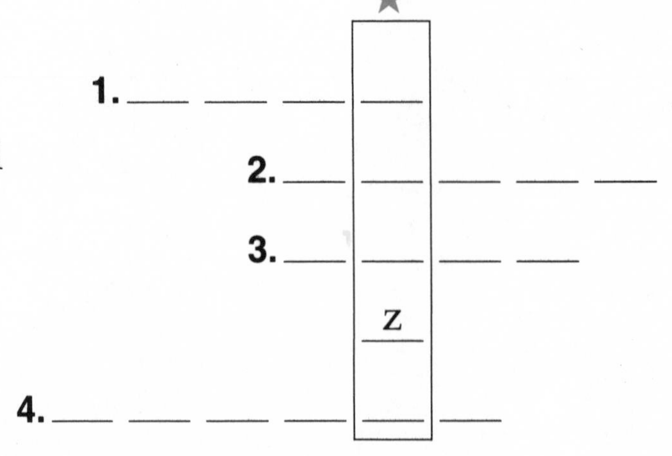

C. Read down from the star at the top of the puzzle. Another name for corn is ________________.

 r-controlled vowel sound-letter correspondences: /är/ *ar*, /ėr/ *er*, *ir*, *ur*, /ôr/ *or*; using vowel sounds to decode words

WHILE YOU READ

Look for the letters ar, er, ir, or, or ur in a word. Use what you know about the sound the vowel followed by r stands for to help you read the word.

A farmer plants corn seeds in the spring. Soon a corn plant starts to grow. At first the plant is short. But by the middle of the summer, the plant can be taller than the farmer.

The ears of a corn plant grow in the summer, too. Each ear has long thin strings along it. The strings stick out at the end. The strings change color as the ear of corn grows. At first they are light yellow. Next they turn dark red. Last, they turn brown. Then it is time for the farmer to pick the ear of corn.

AFTER YOU READ

A. Fill in the circle for the answer.

1. When does a farmer plant corn seeds?

○ in summer ○ in spring ○ in winter

2. An ear of corn is picked when the strings are

○ dark red ○ light yellow ○ brown

3. The story is mostly about

○ colors ○ corn ○ farmers

B. Get some seeds from a store or your teacher. Put soil in a paper cup. Put the seeds in the soil. Water them. See if a plant grows.

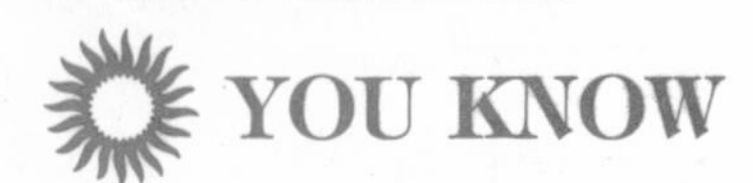

REVIEW

YOU KNOW

- The vowel letters can stand for short or long vowel sounds.
- Sometimes letters like <u>aw</u>, <u>ea</u>, or <u>ou</u> come together in a word.
- Sometimes the letters <u>ar</u>, <u>er</u>, <u>ir</u>, <u>or</u>, or <u>ur</u> come together in a word.

1. Name the picture. Draw a line under the letter or letters that stand for the vowel sound you hear in the picture name.

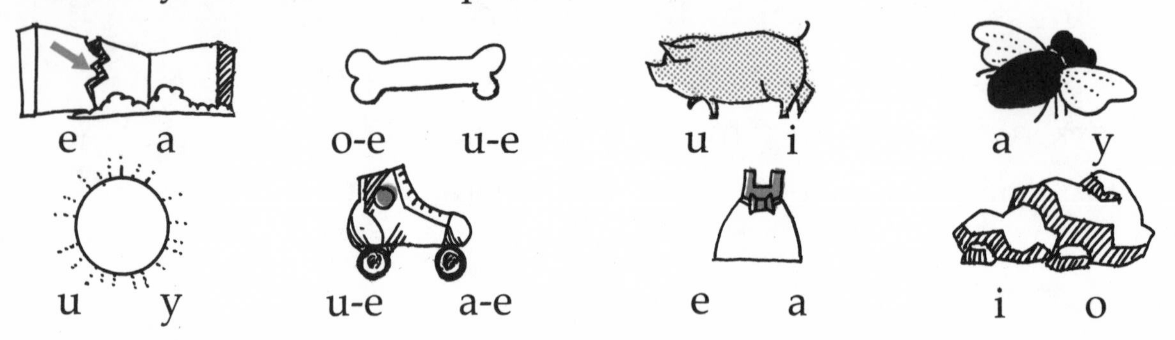

2. Name the picture. Draw a line under the letters that stand for the vowel sound you hear in the picture name.

 Review—short, long, and r-controlled vowel sound-letter correspondences, diphthong sound-letter correspondences; using vowel sounds to decode words

USING WHAT YOU KNOW

Out west are some big white rocks by a cave in the side of a hill. The rocks have marks on them that look like tracks left by the feet of turkeys. People tell a story about these marks.

Long ago, they say, a poor girl lived close by. Her job was to take care of turkeys. She took the turkeys to the rocks by the cave. She stayed with the turkeys all the time.

One day the girl heard about a big party. She wanted to go. But her clothes were worn out. They were just rags. She started to cry.

"Do not cry," the turkeys said to her. "We will help you."

Read clue 1. Find the answer in the box. Write the answer after 1 in the puzzle. Put one letter in each box. Do the same thing for the other clues.

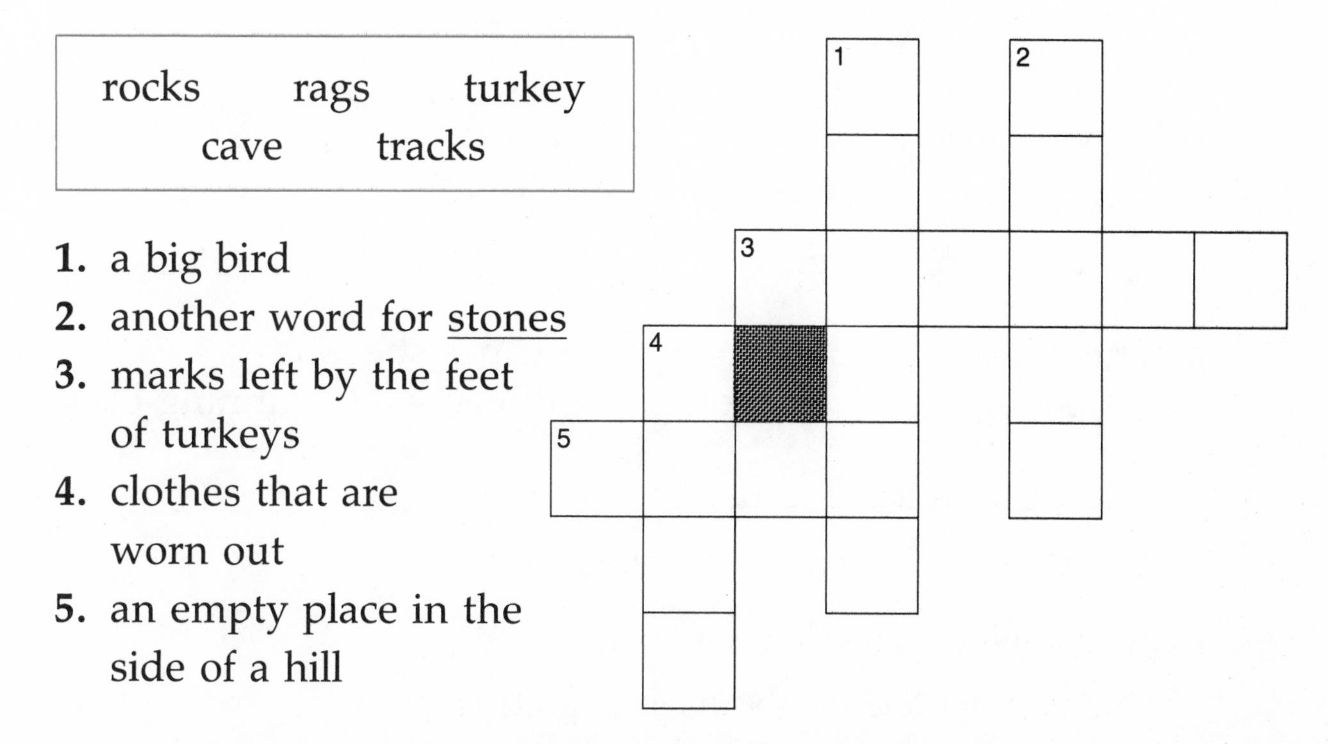

rocks   rags   turkey
cave   tracks

1. a big bird
2. another word for <u>stones</u>
3. marks left by the feet of turkeys
4. clothes that are worn out
5. an empty place in the side of a hill

WHILE YOU READ

Look for letters like a, ee, ir, oi, or ue in a word. Use what you know about the vowel sound for the letter or letters to help you read the word.

To help the girl, each turkey dropped a feather. One feather turned into a blouse. One feather turned into a skirt. Other feathers turned into beads. Soon the girl was ready.

"Have fun," said the turkeys. "But come back to these rocks by the middle of the night."

The girl went to the party. She had so much fun she forgot about the time. It grew late.

The girl ran back to the turkeys. But they were gone. She found only the marks left by their feet. These marks are still on the big white rocks by the cave.

AFTER YOU READ

A. Fill in the circle for the answer.

1. The turkey feathers turned into

○ rocks ○ a girl ○ clothes

2. The girl forgot about the time because she was

○ having fun ○ holding feathers ○ running back

3. The turkeys left because the girl was

○ pretty ○ late ○ happy

B. Draw a picture to go with the story. Write one or two sentences about your picture.

Lesson 14 CUMULATIVE REVIEW

What do you see in the night sky? You may see the moon. You may see many bright stars.

The stars look like tiny white lights. But stars are not tiny. Most of them are not white. Stars only look tiny and white because they are so far away.

Our sun is a star. Some stars are much bigger than our sun. Some are about the same size. Some tiny stars are much smaller than our sun.

Stars are different colors. Very hot stars are blue. Stars that are not very hot are orange or red. Yellow stars, like our sun, are in the middle.

1. What is our sun?
- ○ a ball
- ○ a star
- ○ a moon

2. Stars look tiny because they are
- ○ hot
- ○ white
- ○ far away

3. What does the color of a star show?
- ○ how big it is
- ○ how hot it is
- ○ how far away it is

4. A yellow star is
- ○ hotter than a red one
- ○ cooler than a red one
- ○ hotter than a blue one

5. What is the story about?
- ○ stars
- ○ colors
- ○ the sun

6. How would stars look if they were closer to us?
- ○ all blue
- ○ all white
- ○ all different colors

Not all the lights in the sky are stars. Some are other planets. People have found eight other planets.

Earth is a planet. It goes around the sun. The other planets go around the sun, too.

The other planets are different sizes. Four are about the same size as Earth. Four are giants. In the night sky they all look like stars to us. This is because they are far away.

Earth has one moon that goes around it. Some of the other planets have moons that go around them, too. All of them have more moons than Earth.

7. How many other planets have people found?
- ○ one
- ○ four
- ○ eight

8. The other planets go around
- ○ the sun
- ○ the moon
- ○ Earth

9. The other planets look like stars to us because
- ○ they are lights
- ○ they are far away
- ○ they are different sizes

10. From the story, you know that
- ○ there is only one moon
- ○ Earth has the biggest moon
- ○ some planets have more than one moon

11. How would people act if another planet is found?
- ○ interested
- ○ funny
- ○ hurt

12. Which sentence best tells about the story?
- ○ It is not true.
- ○ It is too short.
- ○ It is about real things.

Maria Mitchell loved to watch things in the sky. She began helping her father watch the sky when she was 12.

One clear night in 1847, Maria stood on the roof. She was watching the sky. She was using a special tool that made things far away look close. This night she saw a strange fuzzy thing that was not on her map of the sky.

Maria called her father. He looked, too. He saw the fuzzy thing Maria saw. Maria had found something new in the sky!

Soon many people knew about the new thing Maria had found in the sky. She won prizes. The King of Denmark even sent her a piece of gold.

13. Maria Mitchell and her father

- ○ made tools
- ○ watched the sky
- ○ found gold on the roof

14. Why was the night in 1847 different?

- ○ It was clear.
- ○ Maria used a new tool.
- ○ Maria found something new.

15. Maria knew what she saw was new because it was

- ○ far away
- ○ not on her map
- ○ strange and fuzzy

16. How do you think Maria's father felt at the end?

- ○ angry at her
- ○ proud of her
- ○ scared of her

17. Which is the best name for the story?

- ○ "A Special Tool"
- ○ "The Gold Prize"
- ○ "Finding Something New"

18. What do you think Maria did on other clear nights?

- ○ She watched the sky.
- ○ She went to bed.
- ○ She won prizes.

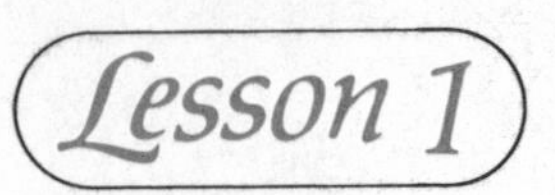

SYLLABLES / READING NEW WORDS

YOU KNOW

- A word can have one vowel sound or more than one vowel sound.
- Each part of a word with a vowel sound is called a syllable.
- Each syllable has one vowel sound.

Say each word to yourself. Listen for the number of vowel sounds and the number of syllables.

go fun eat inside happy monkey

A. Say each word to yourself. Write **1** if you hear one vowel sound. Write **2** if you hear two vowel sounds.

1. grass ______	**4.** picnic ______	**7.** into ______
2. summer ______	**5.** plant ______	**8.** park ______
3. outside ______	**6.** lunch ______	**9.** window ______

B. Say each word to yourself. Write the word in the right list.

	One Syllable	**Two Syllables**
1. carry		
2. ground	______________	______________
3. night		
4. hello	______________	______________

USING WHAT YOU KNOW

Sal woke up at sunrise one morning. She looked out the window. The grass looked as soft as velvet. "This is a perfect day for a picnic lunch," she said to her sister, Ellen. "We can sit on the grass in the park."

The underlined words in the story are words you may not have seen before. Each word has two syllables. If you sound out each syllable, you should be able to read the word.

Here are some things Sal and Ellen found in the kitchen. Which things could they eat at a picnic? Write the things they could eat on the lines in the basket.

muffins	napkins	berries	meatloaf	lantern
raincoat	carrots	scissors	cabbage	walnuts

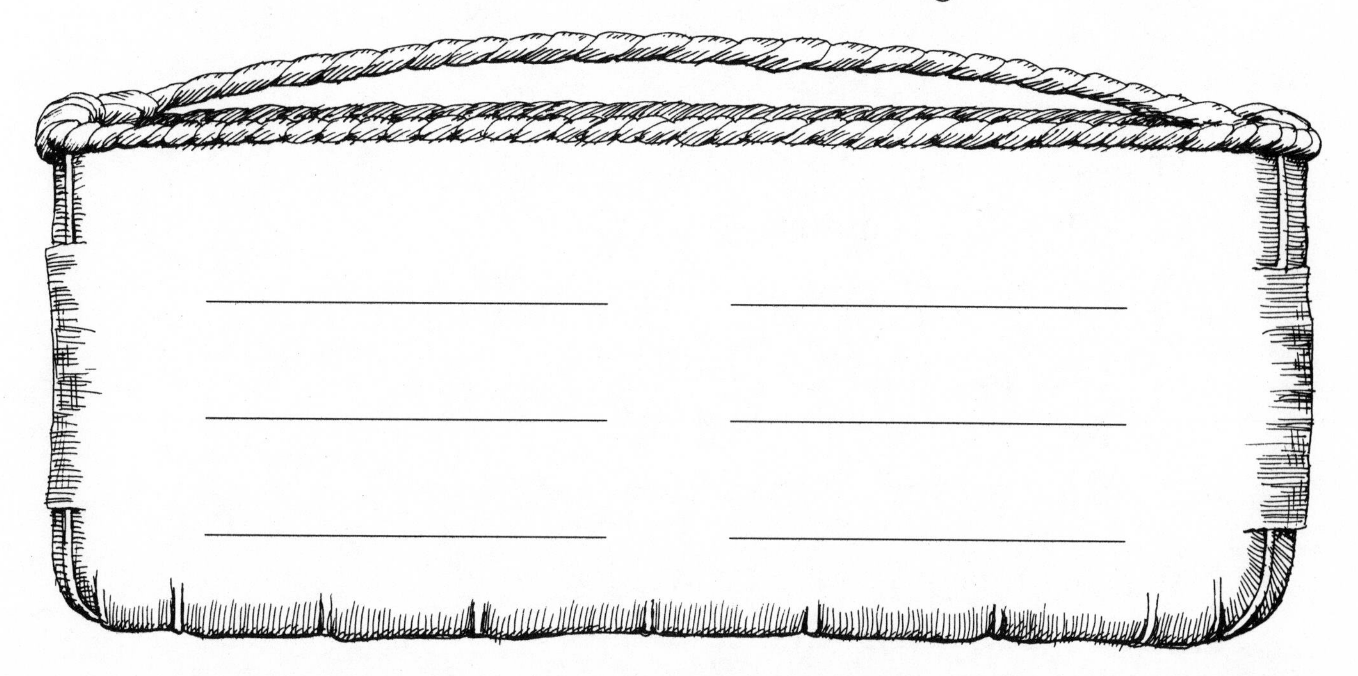

WHILE YOU READ

Sound out each syllable in a word you have not seen before. This will help you read the word.

"I think a picnic lunch would be a mistake," said Ellen. "We would not enjoy it. It will be too hot outside by the time we eat lunch."

Sal looked sad. Then she smiled. "I have a better plan," she said. "This is a splendid morning. Why not welcome the sunrise? We could pack a basket right now and hurry to the park. We could have a picnic breakfast!"

AFTER YOU READ

A. Fill in the circle for the answer.

1. Ellen thought a picnic lunch would be a mistake because

○ it would be too hot outside
○ they would have to hurry
○ she had a better plan

2. The story takes place in the

○ fall ○ summer ○ winter

3. What do you think Sal and Ellen did next?

○ They had lunch outdoors.
○ They went back to bed.
○ They packed a picnic basket.

B. Draw pictures of foods you would like to eat at a picnic. Write the name of each food.

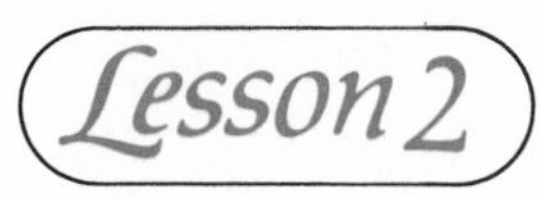

WORD ENDINGS / HOW MANY?

- Adding s or es to a naming word can make it mean "more than one."

Read the word that names each picture.

hat hats dress dresses

A. Look at the picture. Circle the word that names the picture.

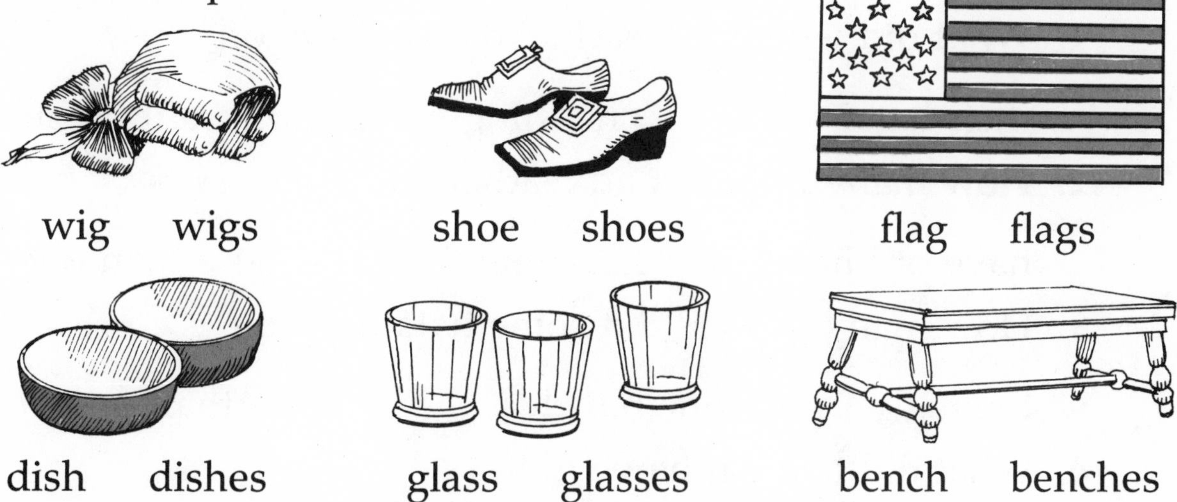

wig wigs shoe shoes flag flags

dish dishes glass glasses bench benches

B. Look at the words you circled in part A.

1. Write the words that name one thing.

__________ __________ __________

2. Write the words that name more than one thing.

__________ __________ __________

USING WHAT YOU KNOW

Women in early America had many things on their hats. Some hats had ribbons and feathers on them. Some hats had bunches of flowers on them. One hat even had a stuffed rooster on it.

To find out how many things are told about in the story, look at the end of each underlined naming word. The ending s or es means there is more than one thing.

A. Put a ✓ in front of the answer.

1. What did women in early America have on their hats? ____ one thing ____ more than one thing

2. How many ribbons and feathers did some hats have on them? ____ one ____ more than one

3. How many flowers did some hats have on them? ____ one bunch ____ more than one bunch

4. What did one hat have on it?

____ one rooster ____ more than one rooster

B. What other things might women in early America have had on their hats? Write them here.

____

____

 Plural noun endings *s, es;* using noun endings to determine how many things are referred to in a sentence

WHILE YOU READ

Look at the naming words in the story. Look for the s and es endings. The endings will help you know how many things are told about in the story.

Many men in early America had beaver hats. These hats were called caps. The men were proud of their beaver caps. They kept them in special boxes.

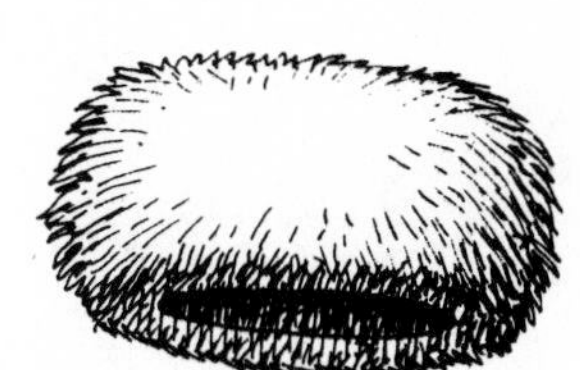

Beaver caps were made from the fur of beavers. The fur might have been part of a coat. When a coat was worn out, some patches were still good. These patches were made into caps.

People thought a beaver cap could make a man think better. This may be why we sometimes say, "Put on your thinking cap!"

AFTER YOU READ

A. Fill in the circle for the answer.

1. What was the story about?

○ one cap ○ many caps ○ two caps

2. Beaver caps were made from worn out

○ patches ○ boxes ○ coats

3. A man who had on a beaver cap might feel

○ old ○ smart ○ hungry

B. Cut out pictures of hats and caps people wear today. Paste them on paper.

Lesson 3 REVIEW

YOU KNOW

- Each part of a word with a vowel sound is called a syllable.
- Each syllable has one vowel sound.
- Adding s or es to a naming word can make it mean "more than one."

A. Say each word to yourself. Write **1** if you hear one vowel sound and one syllable. Write **2** if you hear two vowel sounds and two syllables.

1. clay ______ **3.** pencil ______ **5.** art ______

2. mirror ______ **4.** board ______ **6.** inside ______

B. Look at the picture. Circle the word that names the picture.

box boxes

ladder ladders

can cans

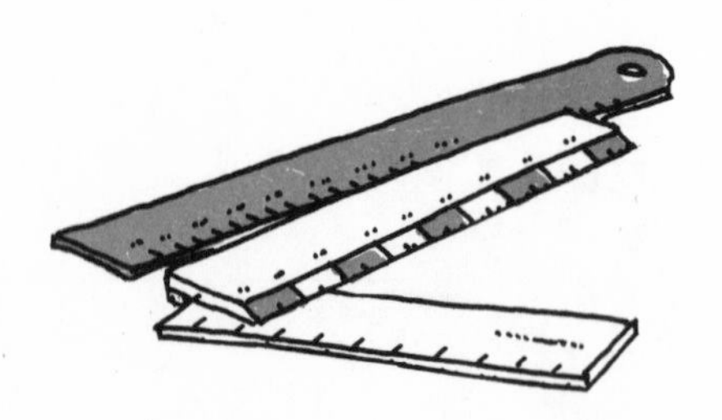

ruler rulers

flower flowers

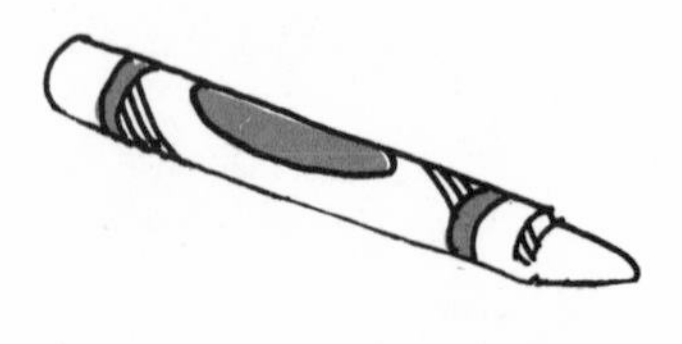

crayon crayons

 Review—syllables, plural noun endings; using syllables to decode unfamiliar words; using noun endings to determine how many things are referred to in a sentence

USING WHAT YOU KNOW

One way of painting a picture is called action painting. Action artists do not use brushes. Instead, they use paints right out of the cans. Most artists cover the floor with canvas or paper. Then they pick colors and drip the paints onto the canvas or paper.

One artist made a strange painting. The artist put plenty of paint on a person. Then the person rolled around on a canvas. The painting did not end up looking like a person!

A. Put a ✓ in front of the answer.

1. Action artists do not use

____ paint ____ brushes ____ canvas

2. How many colors do most artists use?

____ one ____ more than one

3. One artist made a painting using

____ very little paint ____ lots of paint

4. The artist put paint on

____ one person ____ more than one person

B. Color the action painting. Use a different color for each part.

WHILE YOU READ

Sound out each syllable in a word you may not have seen before. Look at the ends of naming words to find out how many things are told about in the story.

Years ago most artists painted pictures that looked real. An artist might have painted a dancer. The dancer looked like a real person.

Later, some artists made pictures using just shapes and colors. Other artists made pictures of real things that did not look real. A face might have eyes in strange places. Dishes might collapse over the edge of a table. People could not always tell what the artist meant to show.

Pop artists today make pictures of real things. But their subjects are very big. They paint things like huge soup cans and giant hotdogs.

AFTER YOU READ

A. Fill in the circle for the answer.

1. What is the story about?

○ one kind of picture ○ many kinds of pictures

2. A person may not be able to tell what an artist meant to show if the artist painted

○ soup cans ○ just shapes and colors ○ real things

B. Think of something small, like a spoon. Draw a great big pop art picture of it.

 Review—syllables, plural noun endings; using syllables to decode unfamiliar words; using noun endings to determine how many things are referred to in a sentence

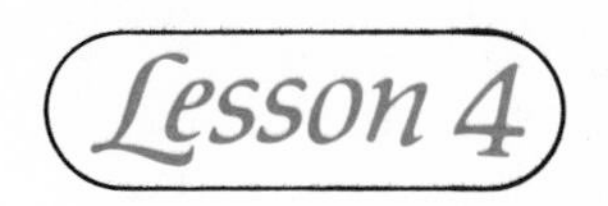

WORD ENDINGS / WHEN THINGS TAKE PLACE

- The ending s, es, ing, or ed can be added to an action word to make another word.

Read the words in each list.

call	push	hop	save	dry
calls	pushes	hops	saves	dries
calling	pushing	hopping	saving	drying
called	pushed	hopped	saved	dried

Circle the word that goes in the sentence.

1. Today our class is ______ a show.
   give gives giving

2. We ______ the other second grade classes.
   invites invited inviting

3. This morning we are ______ everything ready.
   get gets getting

4. Everyone ______ around behind the stage.
   hurry hurries hurrying

5. Pedro ______ from the side of the stage.
   watches watch watching

6. The other classes are ______ into the room.
   come comes coming

7. Soon all the seats are ______.
   fills filled fill

USING WHAT YOU KNOW

1. Pedro turns out the lights. The show is starting. Gina dances across the stage. She rushes back and forth. The people are clapping.

2. Tony tried a magic trick. He dropped a cloth over an empty cage. He waved his hand over it. Then he showed a bird in the cage!

To find out when things in the stories take place, look at the underlined action words. The endings s, es, and ing can tell about things that are happening right now. The ending ed can tell about something that has already happened.

A. Circle the answer.

1. Story 1 tells things that take place now before now

2. Story 2 tells things that take place now before now

B. Read each sentence. Underline the action word. Circle each action word in the puzzle. Look across and down.

1. The band played a march.
2. The children carried flowers.
3. Suzi tosses a ball.
4. A bird flies by.
5. A clown skipped on stage.
6. A dog barks at us.

r	p	e	i	d	p	s	b
f	l	i	e	s	t	s	a
c	a	r	r	i	e	d	r
f	y	e	s	d	r	i	k
o	e	t	o	s	s	e	s
t	d	b	f	l	e	k	e
r	s	k	i	p	p	e	d

WHILE YOU READ

Tip Look at the action words in the story. Look for the s, es, ing, and ed endings. The endings will help you know when things take place.

Dee and Ronnie are clowns. They dressed up in funny clothes before the show. They painted their faces. Now they are running around the stage. Dee is chasing Ronnie. She tosses a pail of water at him. Ronnie ducks. But before the show, Dee filled the pail with paper. So no water comes out. Everyone laughs.

AFTER YOU READ

A. Fill in the circle for the answer.

1. When did Dee and Ronnie dress up?

○ before the show ○ tomorrow ○ after the show

2. No water comes out of the pail because it is filled with

○ paint ○ clothes ○ paper

3. Everyone laughs because the clowns are

○ pretty ○ funny ○ wet

B. Write a name for the story.

____

C. Pretend you are a clown. Draw a picture of yourself doing something funny.

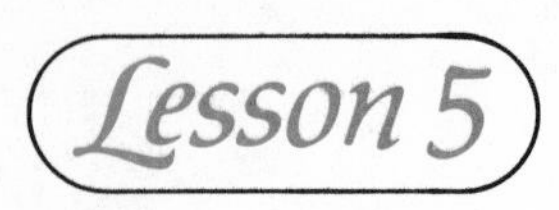

WORD ENDINGS / COMPARING THINGS

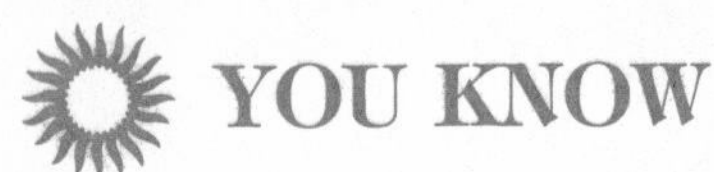

YOU KNOW

- The ending <u>er</u> or <u>est</u> can be added to a describing word to make a new word.

Read the word that tells about each picture.

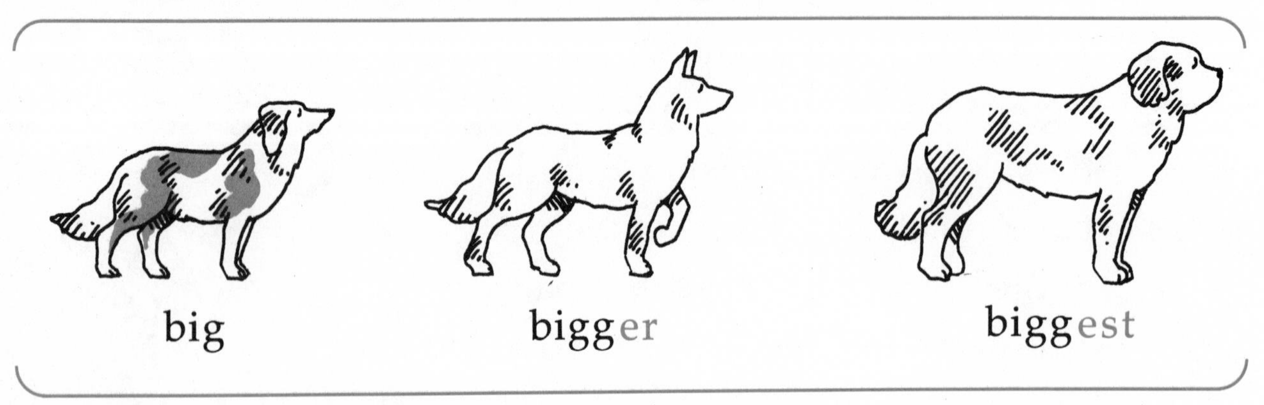

Read the words. Look at the pictures. Write the word that tells about each picture.

1. fast
   faster
   fastest

__________ __________ __________

2. hungry
   hungrier
   hungriest

__________ __________ __________

3. fat
   fatter
   fattest

__________ __________ __________

USING WHAT YOU KNOW

A horse is a tall animal. An elephant is taller than a horse. A giraffe is the tallest animal of all.

To find out how things are different from each other, look at the underlined describing words. The ending er tells how two things are different. The ending est tells how three or more things are different.

A. Look at the picture. Write the word that goes in the sentence.

1. A snake is ______________ than a worm.
longer longest

2. The girl is the ______________ of the three children.
happier happiest

3. The bat kite is the ______________ kite of all.
higher highest

4. The string is ______________ than the rope.
thinner thinnest

B. Look at the ball. Draw a smaller ball next to it.

WHILE YOU READ

Look at the describing words in the story. Look for the <u>er</u> and <u>est</u> endings. The endings will help you know how things in the story are different from each other.

Kangaroos come in many different sizes. But almost all kangaroos have front legs that are shorter than their back legs. Their longer back legs help them hop quickly.

Rat kangaroos are the tiniest kangaroos of all. Gray and red kangaroos are the biggest kangaroos of all. Gray and red kangaroos can make the longest hops of any kangaroos.

AFTER YOU READ

A. Fill in the circle for the answer.

1. Which kangaroos are the tiniest?

○ red kangaroos ○ gray kangaroos ○ rat kangaroos

2. What helps kangaroos hop quickly?

○ their longer back legs
○ their different colors
○ their shorter front legs

3. The story tells about

○ sad things ○ real things ○ noisy things

B. Write four sentences about things in the room. Use words with the <u>er</u> and <u>est</u> endings. You can use words like <u>smaller</u> and <u>highest</u>.

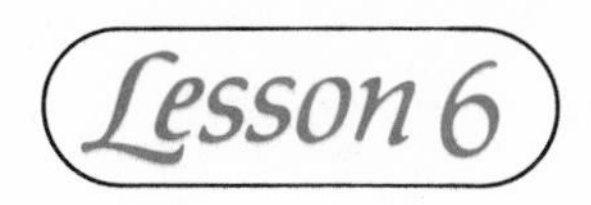

PREFIXES, BASE WORDS / WORD MEANINGS

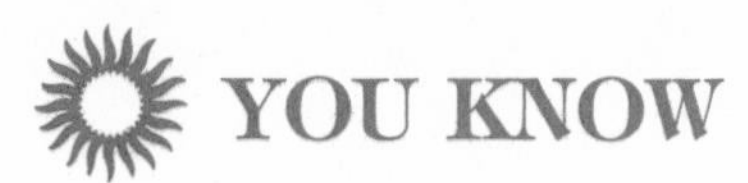

- A prefix is a letter or letters added to the beginning of a base word to make a new word.

Read each prefix, base word, and new word.

Prefix	Base Word	Prefix + Base Word
re	build	rebuild
un	used	unused

A. Add the prefix to the base word. Write the new word.

1. re + read = ____________________

2. un + done = ____________________

3. re + fill = ____________________

4. un + seen = ____________________

B. Read the sentence. Look at the underlined word. Write the prefix and the base word.

	Prefix	Base Word
1. Will you recook the cold food?	_______	____________
2. We are unhappy with this meal.	_______	____________
3. We will leave the food uneaten.	_______	____________

USING WHAT YOU KNOW

Roger put the unwashed dishes in the big machine. He turned on the machine. It made a funny noise and stopped. Then his boss said, "Do not restart that machine. It is not for dishes. It is for clothes!"

Some dishes were unbroken. "I will redo these in the right machine," Roger said.

Each underlined word in the story has a prefix added to a base word. The prefix un can mean not. The prefix re can mean again. Put together the meaning of the prefix and the meaning of the base word to find the meaning of the underlined word.

A. Read the word. Put a ✓ in front of its meaning.

1. unwashed	____ not washed	____ washed again
2. restart	____ not started	____ start again
3. unbroken	____ not broken	____ broken again
4. redo	____ not done	____ do again

B. Draw a picture of an unhappy face. Then redraw your picture. Make the face happy.

 Prefixes and base words: prefixes *re, un;* using the meanings of prefixes and base words to understand the meanings of words

WHILE YOU READ

Look for the prefix re or un at the beginning of a word. Put together the meaning of the prefix and the meaning of the base word.

The Mad Hatter and the March Hare were having a tea party at a big table. Alice went to join them. She sat down. Then she saw that the dishes were unclean.

"You should wash the dishes," Alice said.

"We would just redirty them," said the March Hare. "Then we would have to rewash them. Instead, we just move to new seats."

"Time to move," said the Mad Hatter. They stood up and sat down at new places.

"They were very unfriendly," Alice thought as she left. "I will not revisit them."

AFTER YOU READ

A. Fill in the circle for the answer.

1. The dishes where Alice sat down were
   ○ not pretty ○ clean ○ not clean

2. When will Alice go back to the party?
   ○ never ○ tomorrow ○ often

3. How do you think Alice felt when she left?
   ○ unlucky ○ friendly ○ unhappy

B. Add un to the word able. Add re to the word clean. Use each word in a sentence. Write some things Alice might say to the Mad Hatter.

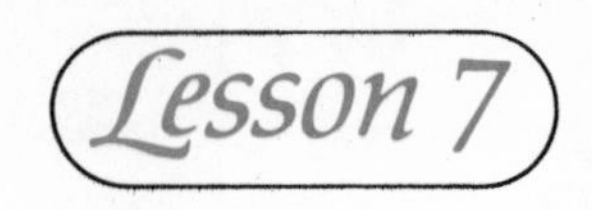

SUFFIXES, BASE WORDS / WORD MEANINGS

- A suffix is a letter or letters added to the end of a base word to make a new word.

Read each base word, suffix, and new word.

Base Word	Suffix	Base Word + Suffix
color	ful	colorful
cloud	y	cloudy

A. Add the suffix to the base word. Write the new word.

1. tear + ful = ____________________

2. wood + y = ____________________

3. hope + ful = ____________________

4. dust + y = ____________________

B. Read the sentence. Look at the underlined word. Write the base word and the suffix.

	Base Word	Suffix
1. Ernie looked in the messy cage.	____________	______
2. He saw something fuzzy.	____________	______
3. It was a wonderful animal!	____________	______

 Suffixes and base words: suffixes *ful, y*; using the meanings of suffixes and base words to understand the meanings of words

USING WHAT YOU KNOW

Ernie picked up the wonderful animal. It was a sandy color. He gave it a playful pat. The animal made a cheerful noise. Then it wagged its bushy tail.

"This is my lucky day," thought Ernie. "I am going to be very careful with my new pet."

Each underlined word in the story has a suffix added to a base word. The suffix ful can mean full of. The suffix y can mean full of or like. Put together the meaning of the suffix and the meaning of the base word to find the meaning of the underlined word.

Read clue 1. Find the underlined word in the story that goes with the clue. Write the word after 1 in the puzzle. Put one letter in each box. Do the same thing for the other clues.

1. like sand
2. full of care
3. full of play
4. full of wonder
5. like a bush
6. full of luck
7. full of cheer

WHILE YOU READ

Tip Look for the suffix ful or y at the end of a word. Put together the meaning of the suffix and the meaning of the base word.

At first Ernie's new pet was just a fluffy ball of fur. Ernie could hold it in his hands. Soon it got bigger. It learned to be helpful. It helped Ernie clean up his room. Ernie was very thankful!

Ernie called his pet Rainy because it loved rainy days. Rainy's fur got full of water when it rained. When Rainy came inside, it shook off its wet fur. The water went all over the place. Mom and Dad said, "Rainy makes it rain inside!"

AFTER YOU READ

A. Fill in the circle for the answer.

1. When Rainy got bigger it was
   ○ careful ○ dirty ○ helpful

2. Rainy made it rain inside by
   ○ shaking off its wet fur
   ○ opening the front door
   ○ going for a walk with Ernie

3. What was the story mostly about?
   ○ the rain ○ a dog ○ Ernie

B. Draw a picture of your pet or a pet you would like to have. Write a name for the pet.

Lesson 8 REVIEW

YOU KNOW

- The ending s, es, ing, or ed can be added to an action word to make another word.
- The ending er or est can be added to a describing word to make a new word.
- A prefix or suffix can be added to the beginning or end of a base word to make a new word.

A. Circle the word that goes in the sentence.

1. The clock bell ______ every hour. ring rings ringing

2. Now it is ______ two times. strike strikes striking

3. An hour ago it ______ once. sounds sounding sounded

B. Read the words. Look at the pictures. Write the word that tells about each picture.

short
shorter
shortest

______________ ______________ ______________

C. Add the prefix or suffix to the base word. Write the new word.

1. re + write = ______________ **3.** joy + ful = ______________

2. un + tie = ______________ **4.** hill + y = ______________

Review—inflectional endings, affixes, base words; using inflectional endings as clues to when events take place and to understand comparisons; using the meanings of affixes and base words to understand the meanings of words

USING WHAT YOU KNOW

One early kind of clock was a candle. Lines marked on the candle showed the hours. People could not reuse this kind of clock.

An earlier kind of clock used sand in a glass jar with two parts. There was a small hole between the parts of the jar. The sand dropped slowly from one part into the other.

The earliest clock of all might be one that used a shadow made by the sun. The shadow fell on lines marked in a circle around a raised piece in the middle. People could not use this clock to tell time on a cloudy day.

A. When was each clock used? Draw a line from the word to the picture of the right clock.

early

earlier

earliest

B. Draw a line under the answer.

1. The clocks in the story were used   now   before now
2. Which clock could not be used again?

3. The earliest clock could <u>not</u> tell time when the sky was   full of sunlight   full of clouds

 Review—inflectional endings, affixes, base words; using inflectional endings as clues to when events take place and to understand comparisons; using the meanings of affixes and base words to understand the meanings of words

WHILE YOU READ

Tip Look at the beginnings and endings of action words and describing words in the story. Use what you know about prefixes, suffixes, and word endings to help you understand the words and what the story is all about.

One kind of clock uses two hands that point to numbers. The oldest clocks with hands were very big. Most towns owned only one big clock. The clock sounded a bell each hour. The bell was very helpful. People did not have to see the clock to know the time.

Later, people made smaller clocks. The smallest clocks were called watches. People looked at their watches to tell the time.

AFTER YOU READ

A. Fill in the circle for the answer.

1. Which clocks were made later?

○ the loudest ○ the biggest ○ the smallest

2. People knew the time without looking at a big clock because it had

○ a bell ○ hands ○ a watch

3. What is the story mostly about?

○ small clocks ○ clocks with hands ○ clocks with bells

B. Find or draw pictures of clocks we use today. Cut them out. Paste them on paper.

Review—inflectional endings, affixes, base words; using inflectional endings as clues to when events take place and to understand comparisons; using the meanings of affixes and base words to understand the meanings of words

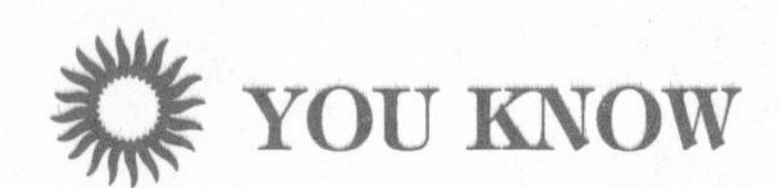

COMPOUND WORDS / WORD MEANINGS

YOU KNOW

- Two small words can be put together to make a longer word.

Look at the words.

back + yard = backyard　　　bed + time = bedtime

A. Choose a word from list 1. Find a word in list 2 that goes with it. Put the two words together. Write the longer word.

1	2	
day	brush	______________
news	work	______________
paint	paper	______________
dog	ship	______________
home	house	______________
space	light	______________

B. Read the word. Draw a line between the two smaller words that make up the word.

1. birthday

2. cookbook

3. bathtub

4. wallpaper

5. playground

6. birdhouse

7. toothpaste

8. snowshoes

 Compound words; using the meanings of the two component words to understand the meaning of a compound word

USING WHAT YOU KNOW

Rosita sat in an armchair in the waiting room. She saw an airplane climb into the sky. Sunlight was shining on its wings. Then she saw a sign light up overhead. The sign said it was time to get on the plane.

Look at the underlined words in the story. Find the two smaller words that make up each word. Put together the meanings of the two smaller words to find the meaning of the underlined word.

A. Write the word that goes in the sentence.

1. An armchair is a ____________ with arms.

2. An airplane is a plane that flies through the ____________.

3. Sunlight is the light of the ____________.

4. Something overhead is ____________ your head.

B. Look at the word. Use letters from the word to make other words. Write the words.

1. storyteller ____________

____

____

2. wintertime ____________

____

____

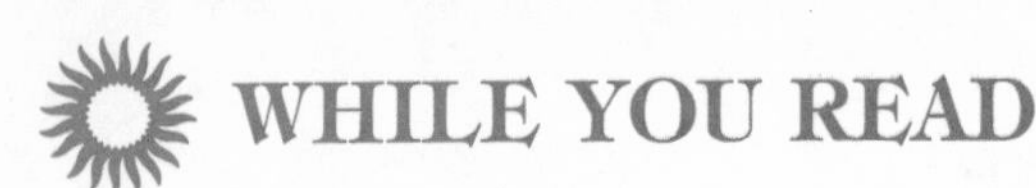

WHILE YOU READ

Look for words made up of two smaller words. Put together the meanings of the smaller words to find out what each longer word means.

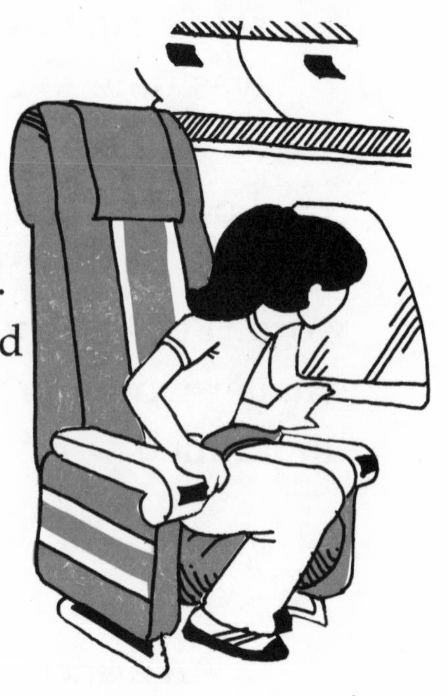

Rosita got on the airplane. She sat down and put her backpack under the seat. Then she put on her seat belt.

The plane rolled down the runway. Soon it was in the air. Rosita looked out the window. The hilltops were right outside. Then she looked down. She saw a tiny world far below. Tiny cars moved on tiny roads past tiny dollhouses.

Rosita fell asleep. It was sunset when she woke up. The plane would be landing soon. Then Rosita would be in her hometown.

AFTER YOU READ

A. Fill in the circle for the answer.

1. What did Rosita see from the window?

○ her house ○ the tops of hills ○ the sunrise

2. Things looked tiny from the plane because they were

○ far away ○ outside ○ for dolls

3. The plane landed

○ near a car ○ in a snowstorm ○ as night came

B. Draw a picture. Show how your school would look from the window of a plane in the sky.

 Compound words; using the meanings of the two component words to understand the meaning of a compound word

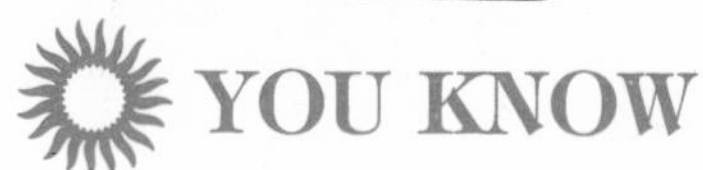

CONTRACTIONS / WORD MEANINGS

YOU KNOW

- Two words can be put together to make a new word by leaving out one or more letters.
- This mark (') takes the place of the letter or letters that are left out.

Read each set of words. The letters in color are left out of the new word.

I am—I'm	we have—we've	it is—it's
you are—you're	can not—can't	they will—they'll
	does not—doesn't	

Read the sentence. Put the two words together. Write the new word. Be sure to use this mark (') for the letter or letters that are left out.

1. ______________ going to a party.
   We are

2. ______________ a birthday party for Tim.
   It is

3. Tim ______________ wait for his friends to come.
   can not

4. He wonders what ______________ bring.
   they will

5. The doorbell rings. ______________ here!
   They are

6. "______________ glad you are here," Tim says.
   I am

7. "______________ everything ready," he adds.
   We have

Contractions with *am, are, have, is, not, will;* using the meanings of the two component words to understand the meaning of a contraction

USING WHAT YOU KNOW

Everyone is watching. "I'm going to blow out the candles on my birthday cake," Tim says. "I've made a wish. But it's a secret. I can't tell my wish to anyone."

Now Tim will open his presents. They're all in boxes. Tim doesn't know what is in them. Do you think he'll get his wish?

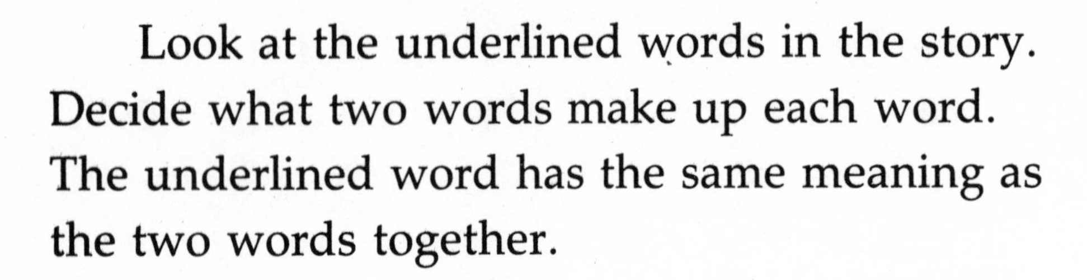

Look at the underlined words in the story. Decide what two words make up each word. The underlined word has the same meaning as the two words together.

A. Read word 1. Find 1 in the puzzle. Write the two words that have the same meaning as word 1. Put one letter on each line. Do the same thing for the other words.

1. he'll
2. don't
3. we're
4. she's
5. we've

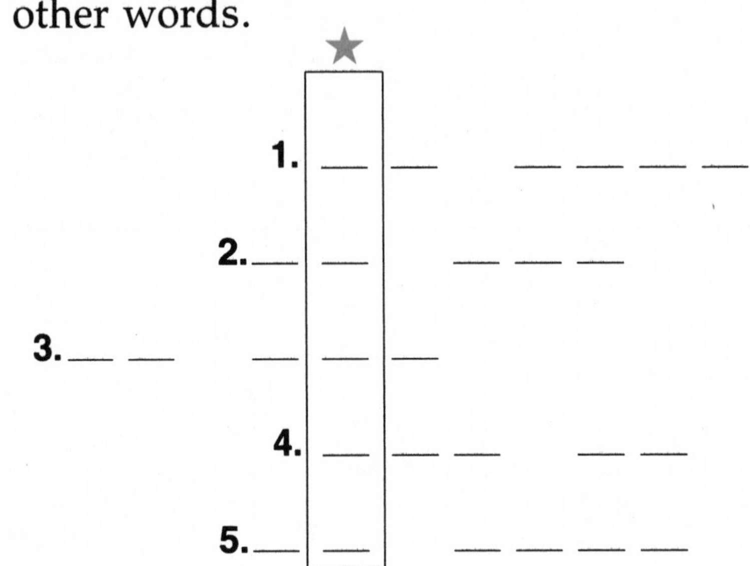

B. Read down from the star at the top of the puzzle. Tim wished for a ____________________.

WHILE YOU READ

Tip Look for words that are made from two words by leaving out one or more letters. The meaning of each word is the same as the meaning of the two words together.

Who Wants a Birthday?

Who wants a birthday?
Somebody does.

"I *am*," says a birthday,
But never "I *was*."

"Five, six," says a birthday:
"You're seven!" "You're nine!"

"I'm yours," says a birthday,
"And you, child, are mine."

"*How* old?" says a birthday.
(You have to guess right.)

"You're *what?*" says a birthday.
(You may be: you *might*.)

"A cake," says a birthday,
"I'm sure there's a cake!"

"A wish," says a birthday,
"What wish did you make?"

"I'm glad," says a birthday,
"To see how you've grown."

"Hello!" says a birthday
("Hello!" says my own.)

–David McCord

AFTER YOU READ

A. Fill in the circle for the answer.

1. What is talking in the poem?
   ○ a guess ○ a wish ○ a birthday

2. The poem is mostly about a
   ○ child ○ birthday ○ cake

B. Copy the sentence. Fill in your own answer. Draw a picture to go with your sentence. "On my next birthday I will wish for ______."

Contractions with *am, are, have, is, not, will;* using the meanings of the two component words to understand the meaning of a contraction

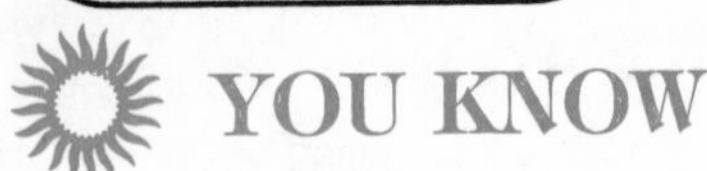

REVIEW

YOU KNOW

- Two small words can be put together to make a longer word.
- Two words can be put together to make a new word by leaving out one or more letters.
- This mark (') takes the place of the letter or letters that are left out.

A. Read the word. Find a word in the box that goes with it. Put the two words together. Write the longer word.

road	made	ball	coat	dog	lace

1. snow ______________ **4.** rain ______________

2. watch ______________ **5.** shoe ______________

3. rail ______________ **6.** home ______________

B. Write the two words as one word. Be sure to use this mark (') for the letter or letters that are left out.

1. he is ______________ **4.** she will ______________

2. they are ______________ **5.** I am ______________

3. have not ______________ **6.** you have ______________

 Review—compound words, contractions; using the meanings of the two component words to understand the meaning of a compound word or a contraction

USING WHAT YOU KNOW

Lucy and her friends were hiking near the hilltops. Lucy stopped at a footbridge to look at a waterfall. When she looked up, her friends weren't there. Lucy listened for footsteps, but she didn't hear any. She looked for footprints on the ground, but she couldn't see any.

"Where could they be?" Lucy said out loud. "I'll have to find them."

A. Read the word. Draw a line to its meaning.

1. hilltops	sounds of feet taking steps
2. footbridge	bridge for people going on foot
3. waterfall	tops of hills
4. footsteps	prints made by feet on the ground
5. footprints	water falling from a high place

B. Here are some things Lucy may say to her friends when she finds them. Write the two words that have the same meaning as the word under the line.

1. I _________________ hear you leave.
didn't

2. _________________ have to come see the waterfall.
You'll

3. _________________ looked all over for you.
I've

4. I think _________________ playing a joke on me.
you're

Review—compound words, contractions; using the meanings of the two component words to understand the meaning of a compound word or a contraction

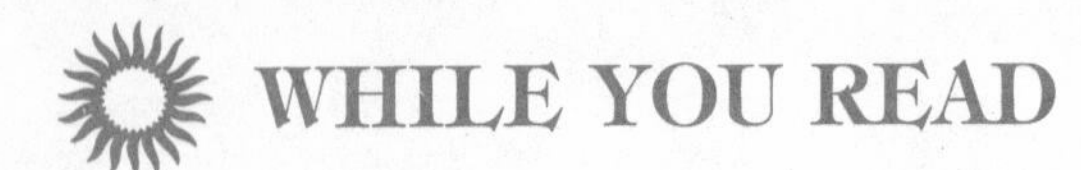

WHILE YOU READ

As you read, look for words that are made up of two words put together. Use the meanings of the two words that were put together to find the meaning of each word.

Lucy set off to find her missing friends. She saw some clouds overhead. "I'm glad I have a raincoat in my backpack," she thought. "I might get caught in a rainstorm."

Lucy walked quickly along the footpath. It wasn't far to the campground. At the campground, the first thing she saw was a fire in the fireplace. Then her friends ran out of the tent.

"Surprise," they shouted. "We've made a campfire. We're going to cook lunch outdoors."

"Lunch cooked over a campfire will be great," said Lucy. "But I hope there isn't a storm!"

AFTER YOU READ

A. Fill in the circle for the answer.

1. Lucy thought there might be a storm with heavy

○ snow ○ rain ○ wind

2. Lucy's friends were missing because they wanted to ______ her.

○ scare ○ write to ○ surprise

B. Draw pictures of foods you would like to cook over a campfire. Circle the one you like best.

 Review—compound words, contractions; using the meanings of the two component words to understand the meaning of a compound word or a contraction

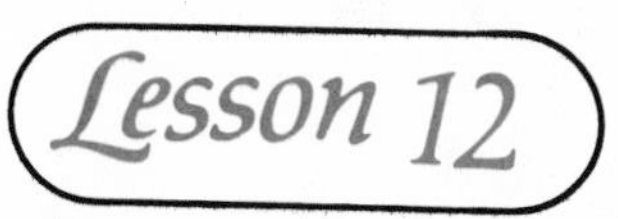

Lesson 12 CONTEXT CLUES / WORD MEANINGS

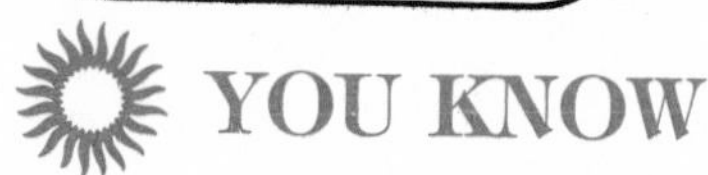

YOU KNOW

- A sentence has clues to the meaning of a word you do not know.

Read the sentence. The underlined words are clues to the meaning of the word in color.

> A castle had a deep moat dug around it and filled with water.

What can be dug deep and filled with water? You can guess that a moat is a kind of hole in the ground.

Read the sentence. Use the underlined words to help you decide the meaning of the word in color. Circle the best meaning.

1. You can see a long way from the site where a castle is built.
   high   place   boat
2. Every castle had a dungeon where bad people were kept.
   jail   bedroom   garden
3. A strong portcullis was slid down to block the way into the castle.
   room   wagon   gate
4. High thick walls kept the castle secure from enemies.
   clean   warm   safe

USING WHAT YOU KNOW

It took many years to build a castle. First a ditch was dug in the earth around the place where the castle would be. Then a strong wooden palisade was built. This was made of tall pointed poles set in the ground. The poles were lashed together with rope. Later, a strong stone wall would take the place of the palisade.

The underlined words in the story are words you may not know. Sometimes the other words in a sentence give clues to the meaning of a word. At other times, you have to look for clues in the other sentences in the story. When you know the meanings of all the words in a sentence, you can understand the sentence.

A. Use the other words in the story to help you decide the meaning of each underlined word. Then write the word that names each picture.

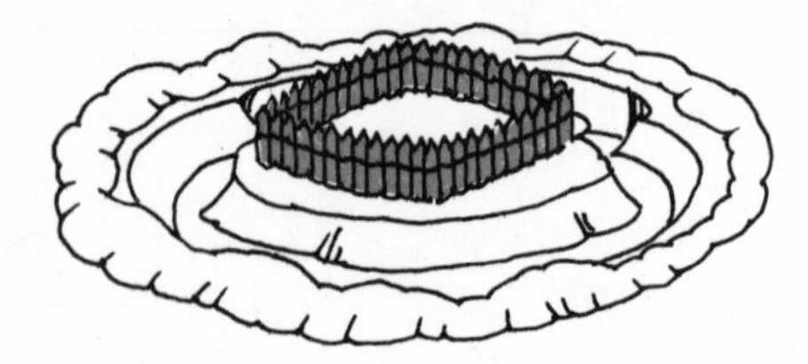

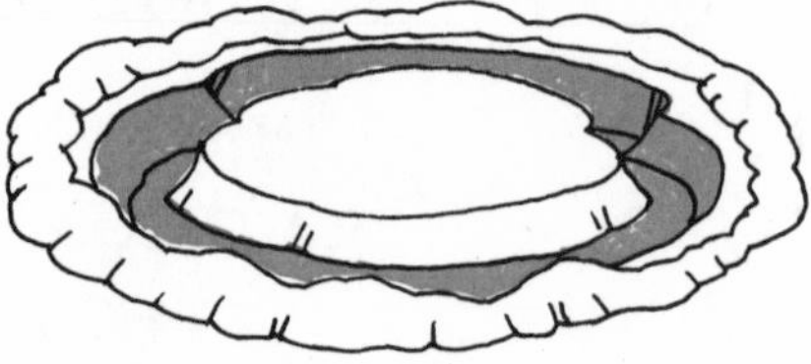

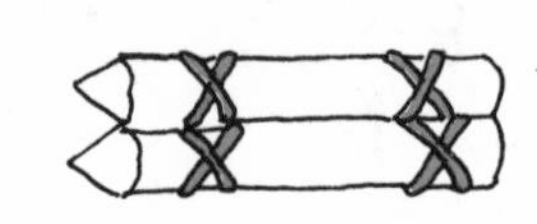

1. ______________ **2.** ______________ **3.** ______________

B. Write the meaning of each word you wrote in part A.

1. ______________ **2.** ______________ **3.** ______________

WHILE YOU READ

Tip Look at the other words in the story for clues to the meanings of words you do not know. The meanings of words help you understand what each sentence is about.

A castle was built to protect the people who lived there. There were tall round towers along the walls. Guards stood high up in the towers to keep watch over the land that surrounded the castle. Attackers had to get past the guards, a moat, and two thick walls.

The lord of the castle and his family lived in the strongest part of the castle. There were rooms full of food. Large cisterns held enough water to last a long time. There was a garden, too. It was not easy for an enemy to make a lord give up his castle!

AFTER YOU READ

A. Fill in the circle for the answer.

1. What is a cistern?

○ a big tub ○ an enemy ○ a thick wall

2. Enemies who attacked a castle would be

○ tall and round ○ seen by guards ○ given food

3. The story is mostly about a

○ garden ○ castle ○ lord

B. Draw your own castle. Don't forget to put guard towers, a portcullis, and a moat in your picture.

Lesson 13 SYNONYMS / WORD MEANINGS

YOU KNOW

- A word can have the same or almost the same meaning as another word.

Read the words that tell about the picture.

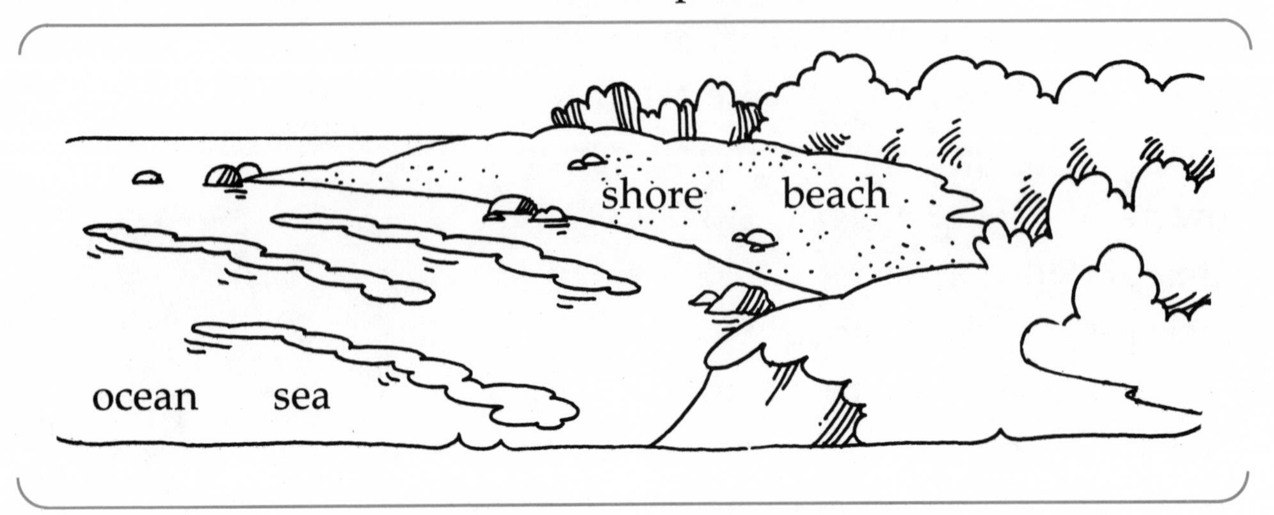

A. Read the first word. Put a ✓ in front of the word with the same or almost the same meaning.

1. under	____ over	____ between	____ below
2. build	____ make	____ sleep	____ bend
3. cap	____ coat	____ hat	____ bed
4. afraid	____ brave	____ scared	____ nice
5. plate	____ store	____ pot	____ dish
6. tired	____ awake	____ sleepy	____ dark
7. soil	____ earth	____ clean	____ snow

B. Read the word. Write a word with the same or almost the same meaning.

1. large __________ **2.** start __________ **3.** glad __________

USING WHAT YOU KNOW

> The <u>heavens</u> are full of stars. From Earth, you can see many stars in the <u>sky</u>.

The underlined words have almost the same meaning. The word you know can help you decide the meaning of the word you do not know.

A. Circle the answer.

1. The heavens are the ______. stars sky
2. Stars are in the ______. heavens Earth

B. Read the sentences. Circle the word that has almost the same meaning as the underlined word.

1. Water covers most of the outside of the planet Earth. So much of Earth's <u>surface</u> is water that Earth should be called Sea!

2. Parts of our world are so dry that no rain falls for years. Not many plants can live in these <u>waterless</u> parts.

3. The top and bottom parts of the Earth have very <u>bitter</u> weather. It is so very cold that all the ice and snow never melt away.

4. It always seems to be summer in the <u>tropical</u> parts of the world. You can see many beautiful flowers in these hot places.

5. People <u>dwell</u> in almost every part of the world. But people do not live in the sea.

WHILE YOU READ

If you do not know the meaning of a word in the story, look for another word with the same or almost the same meaning. This will help you understand what you read.

People can live in many different places. They have clothes, homes, and tools to help them. But most animals can exist only in places that fit their needs. They cannot live in places that are not right for them.

Not many animals can live in the very hot and dry regions of our world. But one kind of toad can live in these places. The toad digs a hole in the ground. It sleeps in the hole until the rains come again.

AFTER YOU READ

A. Fill in the circle for the answer.

1. To exist is to

○ help ○ fit ○ live

2. Where can one kind of toad live?

○ in dry places ○ in deep places ○ in cold places

3. The story mostly tells about where

○ animals live ○ tools are kept ○ people buy clothes

B. Words like hot, dry, and snowy tell about weather. Write a list of words that tell about the weather where you live.

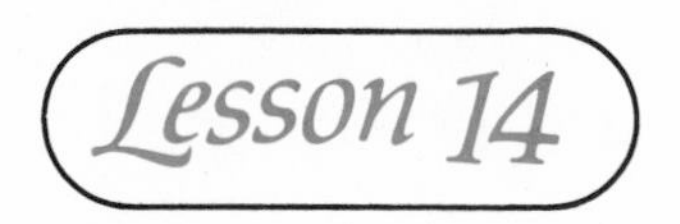

MULTIPLE-MEANING WORDS / WORD MEANINGS

- Some words have more than one meaning.

Read the word that names each picture.

Read the word. Look at the picture. Circle the meaning that the picture shows.

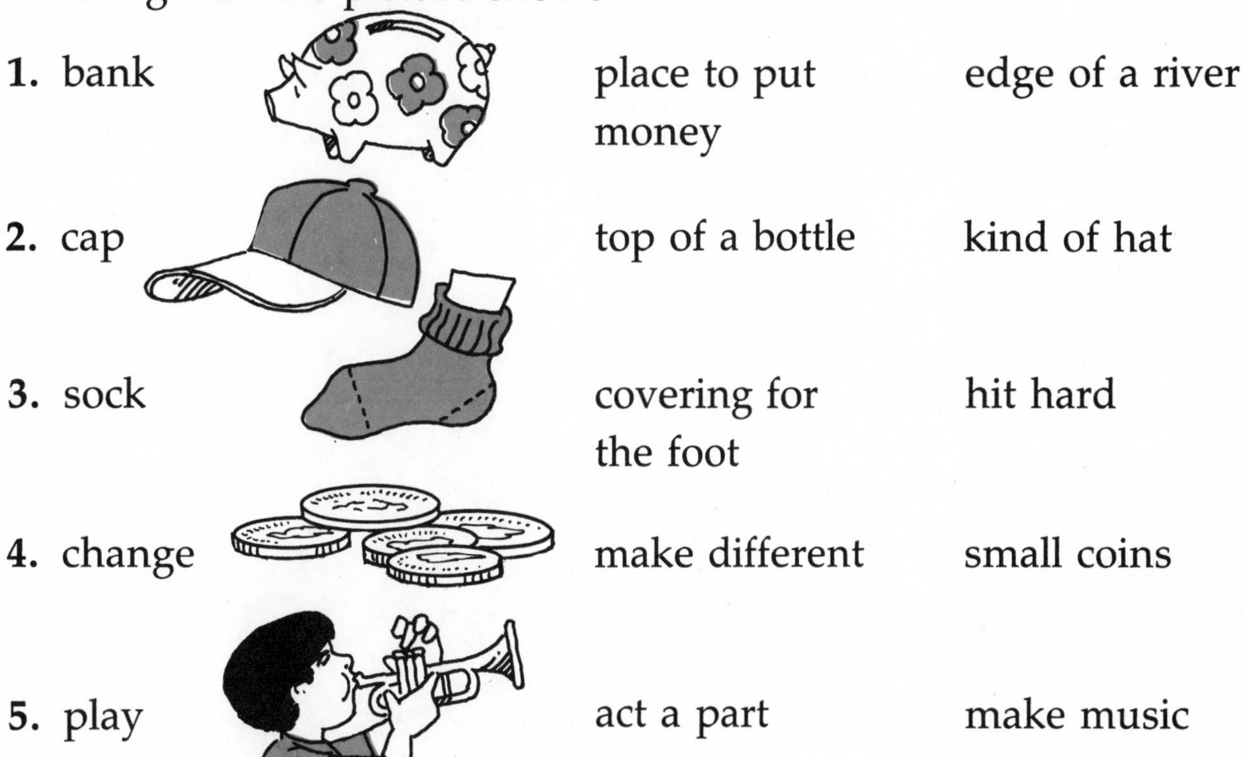

1. bank — place to put money — edge of a river
2. cap — top of a bottle — kind of hat
3. sock — covering for the foot — hit hard
4. change — make different — small coins
5. play — act a part — make music
6. sink — small tub for washing — go down

USING WHAT YOU KNOW

Milly was helping Silly dress to go outside. "This shoe is for your right foot," Milly said.

"Which foot is my wrong foot?" asked Silly.

"You don't have a wrong foot," Milly said. "One foot is your right foot and the other foot is your left foot."

"But both my feet are still here," said Silly.

The underlined words in the story have more than one meaning. The other words in the sentences help you decide which meaning of each word is used.

A. Read the word. Underline the meaning used in the story.

1. dress	put on clothes	piece of clothing
2. right	true	opposite of left
3. foot	12 inches	end part of your leg
4. left	went away	opposite of right

B. Help Silly dress. Draw a shoe on his right foot. Draw a sock and a shoe on his left foot.

WHILE YOU READ

Some words have more than one meaning. Use the other words in the story to help you decide which meaning of a word is used.

Silly was rubbing some stuff on his head.

"Didn't the doctor give you that stuff for your sore arm?" asked Milly.

"Yes," said Silly. "She said it might make my arm smart when I put it on. So I thought I would put it on my head, too!"

AFTER YOU READ

A. Fill in the circle for the answer.

1. The doctor said the stuff might make Silly's arm

○ sleepy ○ bright ○ sting

2. Silly thought the stuff would make him

○ hairy ○ clever ○ sad

3. What might happen next?

○ Silly will get smart.
○ Silly's head will sting.
○ Silly will get angry.

4. This story is

○ funny ○ sad ○ long

B. Pick a word that has more than one meaning. You could use bat, pen, or nail. Draw a picture for each meaning.

Lesson 15 REVIEW

YOU KNOW

- A sentence has clues to the meaning of a word you do not know.
- A word can have the same or almost the same meaning as another word.
- Some words have more than one meaning.

A. Read the first word. Put a ✓ in front of the word with the same or almost the same meaning.

1. fall ____ run ____ hold ____ drop

2. middle ____ top ____ center ____ bottom

3. leave ____ go ____ stay ____ come

4. nice ____ quick ____ kind ____ blue

B. Read the sentence. Circle the best meaning of the underlined word.

1. A raccoon <u>rinses</u> off its food in water before eating it.
washes drinks loses

2. I like to <u>watch</u> birds build their nests.
small clock look at be careful

3. An animal ate a big <u>chunk</u> of the ear of corn.
seed tree piece

4. In <u>spring</u> there are flowers on the trees.
jump up small stream time of year

5. A little <u>shove</u> makes a swing go back and forth.
walk push pass

USING WHAT YOU KNOW

Randy Raccoon went to see his friend Polly Possum. "Hello, Polly," he said. "Will you take a walk with me?"

"Where do we have to take it?" Polly asked. "Is it heavy to carry?"

Randy laughed. "We do not have to carry it. We will just do it. We will stroll along in the park and smell the flowers."

"First, sit down and relax," said Polly.

So Randy sat down with Polly.

A. Read the word. Draw a line to what the word means in the story.

1. see	going on foot
2. walk	rest
3. park	visit
4. stroll	outdoor place
5. relax	walk slowly and quietly

B. Read clue 1. Find the word in the box that goes with the clue. Write the word after 1 in the puzzle. Do the same thing for the other clues.

take	see
smell	sit

1. take a seat
2. get
3. look at
4. sniff at

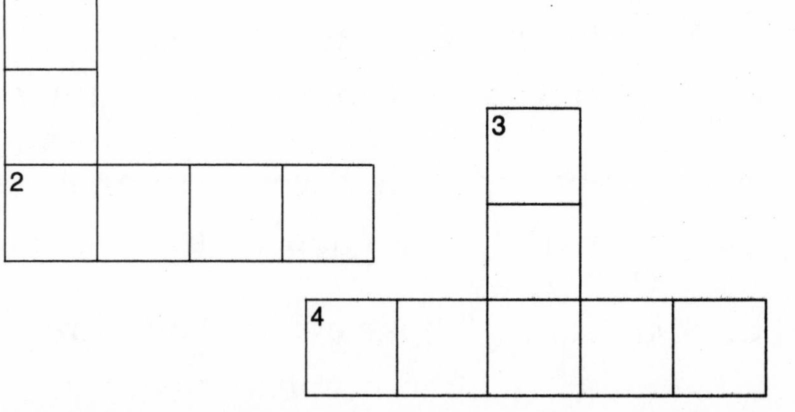

WHILE YOU READ

The story may have words you do not know and words with more than one meaning. Look at the other words in the story for clues to the meanings of these words.

Soon Randy asked, "Have we relaxed long enough?"

"Yes," said Polly. "We can go now."

Randy and Polly walked to the park. A small river ran through it. They stood on a bank and watched as the river flowed by.

"I have a joke to tell you," said Randy. "How do you know a river is rich?"

"I don't know," said Polly.

"Because it has two banks!" Randy answered. He and Polly both laughed.

"That was an amusing joke," said Polly.

AFTER YOU READ

A. Fill in the circle for the answer.

1. The water in the river

○ stood still ○ moved along ○ climbed up

2. Polly thought Randy's joke was

○ right ○ lucky ○ funny

3. Polly and Randy were having a

○ bath ○ good time ○ picnic

B. Read Randy's joke again. Then draw pictures to show two different meanings of the word <u>bank</u>.

Lesson 16 CUMULATIVE REVIEW

Can you write with peanuts? George Washington Carver thought you could. Peanut ink was just one of 300 products he made from peanuts.

Carver spent much of his life making things from crops such as peanuts and sweet potatoes. He thought up new uses for these plants so the farmers who grew them could make more money.

1. What are crops?
   - ⬭ thoughts
   - ⬭ plants
   - ⬭ farmers

2. Why did Carver think up new uses for peanuts and sweet potatoes?
   - ⬭ to get more ink
   - ⬭ to make money
   - ⬭ to help farmers

3. From the story, you can tell that Carver was good at
   - ⬭ thinking up new things
   - ⬭ growing crops
   - ⬭ cooking sweet potatoes

The paper bag has been around for a long time. Margaret Knight invented it in 1867. The paper bags we use today look the same as the bag she made.

Just inventing the paper bag wasn't enough for Knight. She wanted it to be easy for people to make these bags. So she also invented machines for making paper bags.

4. What did Margaret Knight do?
   - ⬭ She lived for a long time.
   - ⬭ She found a paper bag.
   - ⬭ She made new things.

5. Which is the best name for the story?
   - ⬭ "The Paper Bag"
   - ⬭ "The Life of Margaret Knight"
   - ⬭ "New Machines"

6. Why did Knight invent machines for making bags?
   - ⬭ just for fun
   - ⬭ so it would be easy to make bags
   - ⬭ to have enough bags

Long ago people used rags to clean their teeth. Now people use toothbrushes.

A man named William Addis thought rags didn't do a very good job of cleaning teeth. One day he saved some small bones from some food. When they dried, he picked the longest one. He made small holes in it. Then he tied some short animal hairs into tufts. He placed these bunches of hair in the holes in the bone. This was the world's first toothbrush.

---

7. When did people use rags to clean their teeth?

- ⬭ last week
- ⬭ many years ago
- ⬭ yesterday

8. William Addis made

- ⬭ a bunch of clean rags
- ⬭ a tool for making holes
- ⬭ a brush for teeth

9. The brush part of the first toothbrush was made from

- ⬭ broken bones
- ⬭ bunches of hairs
- ⬭ small pieces of food

Kelly was very unhappy. She had lots of things to carry to school, and it was such a rainy day. She couldn't hold all her things and an umbrella!

Then Kelly had an idea. She found an old umbrella and cut the handle short. Then she found an old party hat that had a hard top. She made a hole in the top of the hat and stuck the umbrella in.

Now Kelly was ready. She put on the hat. She went outside and opened the umbrella. Then she walked to school, nice and dry under her umbrella hat.

---

10. A rainy day is

- ⬭ dry
- ⬭ like snow
- ⬭ full of rain

11. Kelly had to carry

- ⬭ many things
- ⬭ one thing
- ⬭ wet things

12. The story was about

- ⬭ a happy day at school
- ⬭ an umbrella hat
- ⬭ a birthday party

People sometimes think up ideas for things that aren't very useful. In the 1500s someone invented a bath bag. If you lived then, this is how you used the bath bag. First you undressed. Then you climbed into the bag and it was tied around your neck. Next, hot water was poured into a hole near the top. The water came out a hole at the bottom. You had to refill the bag with water if you wanted to take a longer bath.

13. To use a bath bag, first you
- ⊂⊃ climbed in
- ⊂⊃ took off your clothes
- ⊂⊃ let the water out

14. If you wanted to take a longer bath you
- ⊂⊃ climbed out of the bag
- ⊂⊃ reheated the water
- ⊂⊃ filled the bag again

15. Most people today would think the bath bag was a ____ idea.
- ⊂⊃ silly
- ⊂⊃ useful
- ⊂⊃ good

Benjamin Franklin invented many things. One of his most useful inventions was called the Franklin stove.

The Franklin stove was better than other ways of heating a room. It gave more heat and it burned less wood.

Franklin never made a lot of money from this invention. Instead, he wanted people to be able to use these stoves without having to pay him for his idea.

16. The Franklin stove
- ⊂⊃ burned too much wood
- ⊂⊃ was good at heating a room
- ⊂⊃ did not give much heat

17. From the story, you know that Franklin was
- ⊂⊃ mean
- ⊂⊃ rich
- ⊂⊃ kind

18. The story told about
- ⊂⊃ a bad invention
- ⊂⊃ a funny invention
- ⊂⊃ a real invention

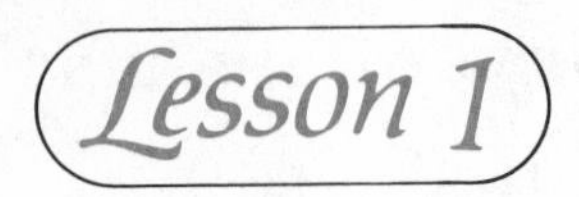

NAMING WORDS, ACTION WORDS / READING LONG SENTENCES

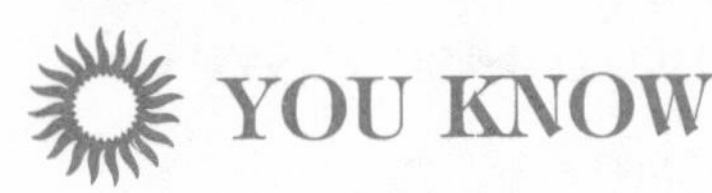

- A naming word names a person, place, or thing.
- An action word tells what a person, place, or thing does or did.

Read each sentence. Look at the naming word and action word.

	Naming Word	Action Word
The girl laughed.	girl	laughed
Run to the lake.	lake	run
A monkey swings about.	monkey	swings
We eat grapes.	grapes	eat

A. Read the words in each row. Circle the naming word.

1. galloped	horse	carry
2. Dennis	sang	jumps
3. ask	town	walked
4. hopped	grow	trees

B. Read the sentence. Underline the action word.

1. The horse galloped away.

2. Dennis jumps rope.

3. I walked to town.

4. The trees grow quickly.

USING WHAT YOU KNOW

A frog hops quickly up the big hill.
A boy chases up the hill after the frog.
Nicole ran ahead and caught the frog in a net.
The girl put the frog in a bag and walked away.

A long sentence often has more than one naming word and more than one action word. The naming words in the sentences above are in color. The action words are underlined. When you read a long sentence, look for naming words and action words. These words help you understand the meaning of the whole sentence.

Read the sentence. Draw a line to the part of the picture that goes with the sentence.

1. The park opened early this morning.
2. Carlos drinks water that he poured from a jar.
3. The branch of the tree bends because so many animals sit on it.
4. A rabbit hid under a big bush.

WHILE YOU READ

Look for naming words and action words. These words will help you understand long sentences.

The Rabbit

When they said the time to hide was mine,
I hid back under a thick grape vine.

And while I was still for the time to pass,
A little gray thing came out of the grass.

He hopped his way through the melon bed
And sat down close by a cabbage head.

He sat down close where I could see,
And his big still eyes looked hard at me,

His big eyes bursting out of the rim,
And I looked back very hard at him.

–Elizabeth Madox Roberts

AFTER YOU READ

A. Fill in the circle for the answer.

1. What did the person in the poem do?
○ hop ○ run ○ hide

2. The little gray thing was a
○ cabbage ○ rabbit ○ bug

3. What game was the person playing?
○ 20 questions ○ hide-and-seek ○ jump rope

B. Read the poem with a friend. Take turns reading two lines at a time.

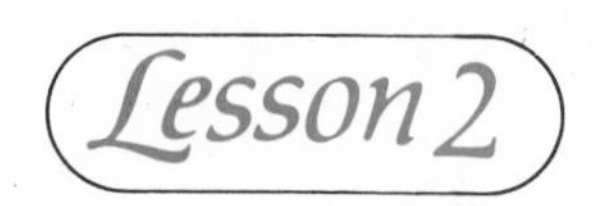

DESCRIBING WORDS / LEARNING ABOUT NAMING WORDS

- A describing word tells about a naming word.

Read the words that tell about each picture.
Each underlined word is a describing word.

strong man   striped tiger   tall clown   big tent

A. Look at the picture. Write a describing word for the naming word under the picture. Use a word from the box.

sad	round
wet	tiny

1. ________________ clown

3. ________________ face

2. ________________ car

4. ________________ body

B. Read the words. Underline the describing word.

1. loud music
2. three tents
3. wild animals
4. happy children

USING WHAT YOU KNOW

Everyone looks up at the high wire. A brave woman walks on the long thin wire. She carries a red and blue umbrella. She dances across the wire to a safe place on the side.

Look at the underlined describing words in the sentences. Each describing word tells something about a naming word. When you read, describing words help you learn more about a person, place, or thing in a sentence.

A. Write the describing word or words from the story that go in the sentence.

1. The wire is ____________ up.

2. The woman is ____________.

3. The wire is ____________ and ____________.

4. The umbrella is ____________ and ____________.

5. The woman goes to a ____________ place.

B. Look at the words you wrote in the sentences in part A. Find each word in the puzzle. Look across and down. Circle each word.

b	r	a	v	e	h	t
l	o	n	g	r	i	h
u	s	a	f	e	g	i
e	s	b	t	d	h	n

 Adjectives; using adjectives to find out more about a person, place, or thing in a sentence

WHILE YOU READ

Look for describing words as you read. They will help you learn more about the people, places, and things in the story.

You can see many clever tricks at a circus. You may see a very tall man with very long legs. You may see a woman eat hot fire.

The tall man's legs are not really so long. He is standing on two long poles. His funny striped pants cover the poles.

The fire eater does not really eat fire. She holds the fire in front of her open mouth. Then she blows out air. Her breath puts out the fire. She does this so quickly you cannot see it happen.

AFTER YOU READ

A. Fill in the circle for the answer.

1. Which word tells about the tall man's poles?
   ○ striped ○ one ○ long

2. The fire goes out because the fire eater
   ○ blows on it ○ is clever ○ cannot see it

3. The story is mostly about
   ○ tall people ○ circus tricks ○ eating fire

B. Draw a picture to tell people the circus is coming. Draw your favorite circus person or animal. Write the word <u>Circus</u> and the date the circus is coming.

Lesson 3 REVIEW

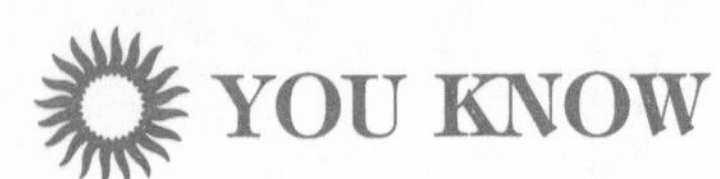

YOU KNOW

- A naming word names a person, place, or thing.
- An action word tells what a person, place, or thing does or did.
- A describing word tells about a naming word.

A. Read the words in each list. Underline the naming word.

1.	**2.**	**3.**	**4.**
big	ran	mother	moved
elephant	blue	helps	five
ate	wet	many	chairs
strong	river	went	soft

B. Read the sentence. Underline the action word.

1. The elephant ate slowly.

2. The river ran for miles.

3. My mother went to work.

4. We moved the chairs.

C. Read the words that tell about the picture. Underline the describing word.

white bear

three turtles

huge elephant

 Review—nouns, verbs, adjectives; using nouns and verbs to understand long sentences; using adjectives to find out more about a person, place, or thing in a sentence

USING WHAT YOU KNOW

Jojo and Bobo were big elephants. Jojo lived in Africa. Bobo lived in Asia. They were both elephants, but they looked different.

Jojo's skin was dark gray. Bobo's skin looked much lighter. Bobo was light gray, and pink spots covered its back.

Jojo's ears grew very long. Bobo's ears did not grow so long. Bobo's ears measured about half the size of Jojo's ears.

How were Jojo and Bobo alike? They both weighed a lot, and they both lifted very heavy things with their trunks.

Read each group of words. Write the words after the name of the right elephant. You can use some of the words more than once.

1. big elephant
2. dark gray
3. lived in Asia
4. weighed a lot
5. lived in Africa
6. light gray
7. pink spots
8. lifted heavy things
9. very long ears

Jojo ______________________

____

____

____

Bobo ______________________

____

____

____

WHILE YOU READ

Tip Look for naming words, action words, and describing words. These words will help you learn about the people, places, and things in the story.

Some young elephants in Asia go to school. They spend seven years there. These elephants learn to follow orders so they can do hard work. They lift and pull heavy logs. They carry heavy things on their backs or with their long trunks.

One trainer stays with each young elephant at a school. The trainer feeds and cares for the elephant. When the elephant leaves the school, the trainer goes, too. A trainer and an elephant may work together all their lives.

AFTER YOU READ

A. Fill in the circle for the answer.

1. Elephants that go to school are

○ seven ○ young ○ heavy

2. To do hard work, elephants must learn to

○ carry things ○ follow orders ○ leave school

3. From the story, you know that a trainer

○ sells elephants ○ draws elephants ○ likes elephants

B. List the things an elephant learns in school. Then list some things you learn in school. Circle any things you wrote in both lists.

Lesson 4 PRONOUNS, ADVERBS / WHAT THEY STAND FOR

YOU KNOW

- Some words can stand for other words.

Read each sentence. The underlined word stands for the word or words in color.

> Mom and Dad said they would take the family on a trip.
>
> "We will go to the mountains because we have never been there before," said Mom.

Circle the word or words the underlined word stands for in the sentence.

1. The Alperts got into their car.
2. Mom pointed to the back seat and said, "Carol and Eddie, sit there."
3. The car had lots of things in it.
4. The children had toys to keep them busy.
5. There was a big box with food in it.
6. The children shouted, "We are leaving!"
7. Then Dad said he had forgotten something.
8. He went back to the house for the thing he had left there.
9. Dad came back with the car keys in his hand.

USING WHAT YOU KNOW

Dear Aunt Donna,

1. We are in the mountains. 2. It is beautiful here. 3. The mountains are white on top. 4. They are covered with snow there. 5. Last night a raccoon tried to get our food. 6. But it couldn't open the box. 7. It has a good lock.

Love,
Carol

Ms. Donna Alpert
10 Park Street
Deep River, CT 06417

Look at the underlined words in the letter. Sometimes the words they stand for are not in the same sentence. Look at the words around each underlined word to find the word or words it stands for in the letter.

A. Write the answer.

1. In sentence 2, here stands for ______________________.

2. In sentence 4, They stands for ______________________.

3. In sentence 4, there stands for ______________________.

4. In sentence 6, it stands for ______________________.

5. In sentence 7, It stands for ______________________.

B. Rewrite sentence 2 below. Use there or she to stand for the underlined word or words.

1. Carol finds the lake. **2.** Carol swims in the lake.

____

 Pronoun and adverb referents; recognizing the word or words to which a pronoun or an adverb refers; using pronoun and adverb referents to understand sentences

WHILE YOU READ

When you see words like it, he, and there, look for the words they stand for in the story. This will help you understand what you read.

Dear Aunt Donna,

Eddie didn't have a very good day yesterday. First he fell into the lake. Then he was chased by some bees. They didn't get him. At dinner his food fell into the fire. Finally Eddie said, "I'm going to bed so nothing else happens to me." Then the tent fell down. Eddie was in there when it happened!

Love,
Carol

Ms. Donna Alpert
10 Park Street
Deep River, CT 06417

AFTER YOU READ

A. Fill in the circle for the answer.

1. Where was Eddie when the tent fell down?

○ in the lake ○ in the fire ○ in the tent

2. At the end of the day, Eddie was

○ sleepy ○ unhappy ○ lucky

3. What was Carol's letter about?

○ a bad day ○ a wet day ○ a good day

B. You can hike, fish, swim, and go for a boat ride in the mountains. Write a letter to a friend. Tell what you do in the mountains.

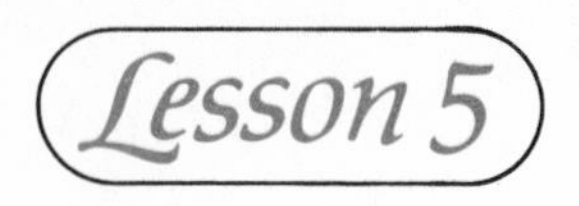

DIRECTIONS / FOLLOWING STEPS IN ORDER

- Directions tell you how to do things.

Read the directions.

1. Open a can of cat food.
2. Put the food in a bowl.
3. Put the bowl on the floor.

A. What do the directions tell you how to do?
Put a ✓ in front of the answer.

_____ wash a cat food bowl

_____ get food ready for a cat

_____ buy a can of cat food

B. Read the directions.

1. Take the bottom off an empty small can and cover the rough edges with tape.
2. Put one end of the can into soapy water.
3. Lift up the can and blow through the end that was not in the water.

What do the directions tell you how to do?
Put a ✓ in front of the answer.

_____ open a can of bubbles

_____ take a bubble bath

_____ make a bubble blower

USING WHAT YOU KNOW

1. Get two empty tall juice cans and two long pieces of heavy string.
2. Punch two holes in the bottom of each can.
3. Put one piece of string through the two holes in each can.
4. Tie the ends of each string together.
5. Stand on top of the cans and pull the strings tight. Then walk.

When you see directions, read them carefully. Then follow all the steps in order so that you do things right.

A. Three children tried to follow the directions at the top of the page. Underline the picture of the child who followed all the steps in order.

B. Follow the directions.

1. Put your pencil on dot A.
2. Draw a line from A to B.
3. Keep drawing lines from dot to dot in ABC order.
4. Write the name of what you drew on the line.
5. Draw a fish in it.

____

WHILE YOU READ

Read directions in a story carefully. See if all the steps were followed in order. This will help you know if things were done right.

Elena followed these steps to make a rock turtle. 1. Find a big round rock and five little flat rocks. 2. Glue one little rock near the edge of the big rock. Let the glue dry. 3. Turn over the rock. 4. Glue the four little rocks at different places on the big rock. Let the glue dry. 5. Paint the rocks to look like a turtle.

Elena had a cute rock turtle. One little rock was its head. The other four little rocks were its feet. She named it Rocky.

AFTER YOU READ

A. Fill in the circle for the answer.

1. What was the last step in making a rock turtle?

○ find the rocks ○ paint the rocks ○ glue the rocks

2. The big round rock was the turtle's

○ head and tail ○ arms and feet ○ body and shell

3. From the story, you know that Elena

○ followed all the steps in order

○ forgot to glue on the little rocks

○ did not have any paint

B. Make a rock turtle, or draw a picture of one. Follow the directions in the story.

Lesson 6 REVIEW

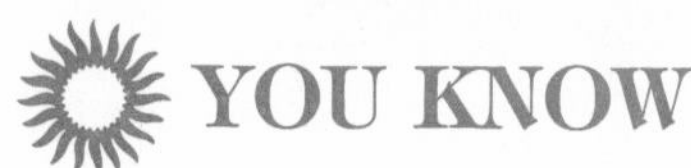

YOU KNOW

- Some words stand for other words.
- Directions tell you how to do things.

A. Circle the word or words the underlined word stands for in the sentence.

1. Aldo made prints of <u>his</u> fingers.
2. First Aldo got white paper and put <u>it</u> on a table.
3. Then Aldo put ink on his fingers and pressed <u>them</u> onto the paper.
4. When Aldo lifted his fingers from the paper, his prints were <u>there</u>.
5. Aldo's friends said <u>they</u> wanted to make prints, too.

B. Read the directions.

1. Put ink on your thumb.
2. Press it onto paper.
3. Draw lines with a crayon or a pencil to make a picture.

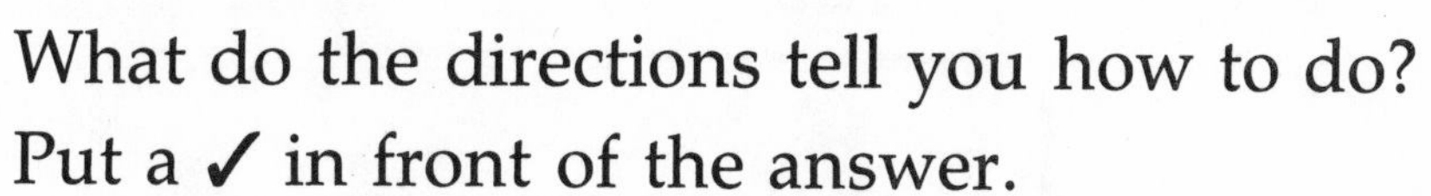

What do the directions tell you how to do?
Put a ✓ in front of the answer.

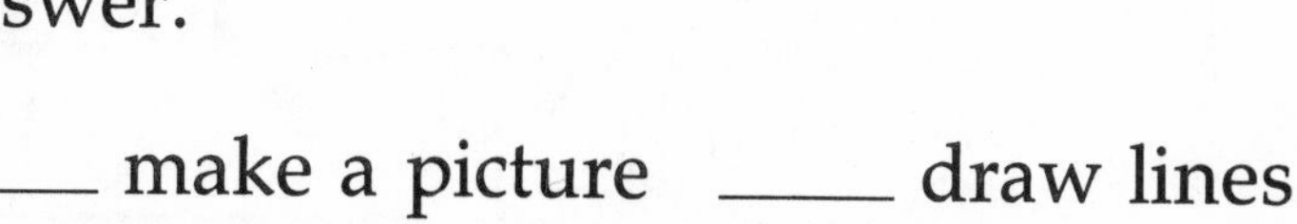

_____ ink your thumb _____ make a picture _____ draw lines

USING WHAT YOU KNOW

1. You don't have to use ink to make prints. 2. You can make them with clear tape. 3. Take a piece of tape. 4. Put the tip of your finger on the sticky side. 5. Your print will stay there when you lift up your finger. 6. Hold the tape up to a light. 7. You will see your print on it.

A. Write the answer.

1. In sentence 2, them stands for ________________.

2. In sentence 5, there stands for ________________.

3. In sentence 7, it stands for ________________.

B. Read the directions. Follow them to find out who did it.

1. Look at the print on the fruit bowl.
2. Draw a line to the first set of prints.
3. Find the print there that matches the one on the bowl.
4. Draw a line on that path to the next set of prints.
5. Follow steps 3 and 4 again.

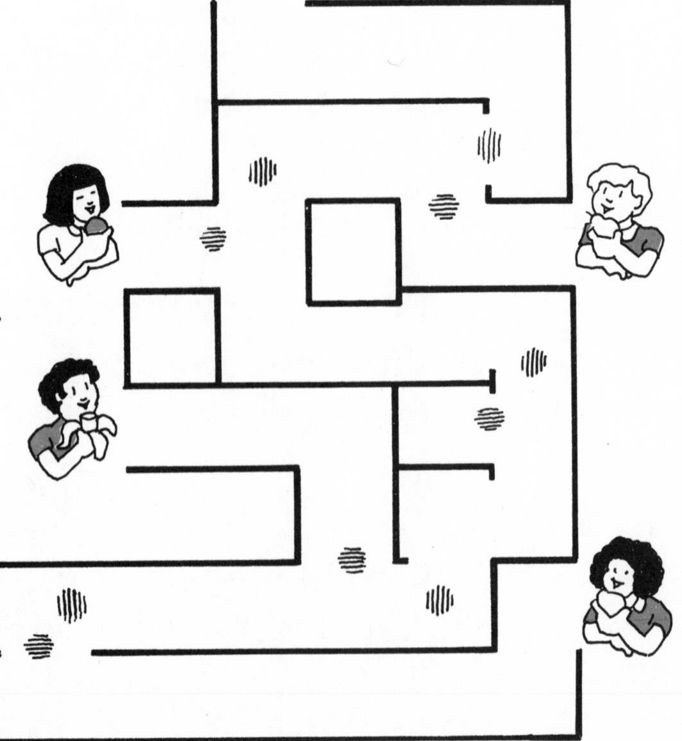

 Review—pronoun and adverb referents, directions; using pronoun and adverb referents to understand sentences; recognizing that all the steps in directions should be followed in order

WHILE YOU READ

When you see words like it and here, look for the words they stand for. When you read directions, see if all the steps were followed in order. These things will help you understand what you read.

Kim was reading a book. It said no two people have exactly the same fingerprints.

"It says here we have different fingerprints," Kim said to Nate. "Let's find out if it's true."

To find out, both Kim and Nate followed these steps. 1. Pick a finger. 2. Make a print of it on tape. 3. Hold the tape up to a light and look at the lines and shapes. 4. Hold your friend's print next to yours. See if the lines and shapes are the same or different.

"It's true," said Kim and Nate.

AFTER YOU READ

A. Fill in the circle for the answer.

1. Where did Kim find out about fingerprints?

○ on the tape ○ in a book ○ on Nate's finger

2. Kim and Nate had ______ fingerprints.

○ different ○ the same ○ dirty

B. Make prints of your fingers. Follow the directions at the top of page 110. Look at your prints next to a friend's. Look for the different lines and shapes.

Review—pronoun and adverb referents, directions; using pronoun and adverb referents to understand sentences; recognizing that all the steps in directions should be followed in order

Lesson 7 PUNCTUATION / HOW TO READ SENTENCES

YOU KNOW

- A sentence that shows surprise or strong feeling ends with this mark (!).
- These marks (" ") are used around the exact words a speaker says.

Look at the picture and read what each animal said. The sentences under the picture have these marks (" ") to show the exact words each animal said.

Chicken Little cried, "The sky is falling!"

"We must get help!" said Henny Penny.

Read each sentence. Put a ✓ in front of the sentence if it shows surprise or strong feeling. If the sentence shows the exact words an animal said, underline those words.

1. _____ A nut hit Chicken Little on the head!
2. _____ "The sky is falling!" cried Chicken Little.
3. _____ Chicken Little told Henny Penny, "The sky is falling."
4. _____ Henny Penny said, "We must get help!"
5. _____ "Yes, we must," said Chicken Little.

USING WHAT YOU KNOW

"What is wrong?" asked Goosey Loosey.
"The sky is falling!" cried Chicken Little.
"A big piece of it hit me on the head!"
"What can we do?" asked Goosey Loosey.
"Let's go tell the king!" said Henny Penny.

Look at the marks at the beginning and end of each sentence. They help you know how to read the sentence. Read a sentence with this mark (!) to show surprise or strong feeling. Read a sentence with these marks (" ") to find out exactly what the speaker said.

A. Put a ✓ in front of two answers.

1. Which animals said things that showed strong feelings?

_____Goosey Loosey _____Chicken Little _____Henny Penny

2. What two things did Goosey Loosey say?

_____"What is wrong?" _____"Let's go tell the king!"
_____"The sky is falling!" _____"What can we do?"

B. The animals met Ducky Lucky. Write what you think Ducky Lucky may say when she finds out what happened to Chicken Little. Use these marks (!) (" ") in your sentence and the words said Ducky Lucky at the end.

____

____

Exclamation mark, quotation marks; using an exclamation mark to understand how to read an exclamatory sentence; using quotation marks to determine a speaker's exact words

WHILE YOU READ

To understand the meaning of a sentence, look at the marks at the beginning and the end. The marks will tell you how to read the sentence.

The animals met Foxy Loxy.

"Where are you going?" Foxy Loxy asked.

"We must find the king," said Henny Penny.

"The sky is falling!" cried Chicken Little.

"I know where the king is," said Foxy Loxy. Foxy Loxy led the animals to his own den. "The king is in there," Foxy Loxy said.

All the animals went into the den. Foxy Loxy followed them in. Foxy Loxy was the only one that ever came out!

AFTER YOU READ

A. Fill in the circle for the answer.

1. What did Henny Penny say?

○ "The king is in there."

○ "I know where the king is."

○ "We must find the king."

2. At the end, Foxy Loxy

○ ate the animals ○ went to sleep ○ saw the king

3. The end of the story was a

○ gift ○ surprise ○ magic trick

B. Write some rhyming animal names.

 Exclamation mark, quotation marks; using an exclamation mark to understand how to read an exclamatory sentence; using quotation marks to determine a speaker's exact words

Lesson 8 COMMAS / THINGS IN A LIST

YOU KNOW

- A comma (,) is used between words in a list.

Read the sentences. Commas are used between the animal names in each list.

> Farmer Hill has cows, chickens, and pigs on her farm.
>
> Farmer Santos has goats, sheep, ducks, and horses on his farm.

A. Read each sentence. Underline the sentence if it has words in a list.

1. Farmers grow the food we eat.
2. We get vegetables, fruit, and meat from farms.
3. Some vegetables are potatoes, peas, carrots, and corn.
4. Oranges, apples, and bananas grow on trees.
5. Cheese and butter are made from fresh milk.
6. Some people eat the meat of chickens, pigs, and cattle.

B. Finish the sentence below. List three things you could see on a farm. Use your own words or some of the words above. Put commas between the words in the list and before the word and.

I went to a farm. I saw ______________________________

____

USING WHAT YOU KNOW

1. Chickens, ducks, and geese lay eggs.
2. Carrots, potatoes, and peanuts grow under the ground.
3. A farmer does not like mice, rabbits, or crows because they eat plants.

When you see a sentence with a list of things, commas help you know what the different things in the list are.

A. Look at each sentence above. Find the things that are listed. Write them below.

1. Sentence 1 ____________ ____________ ____________

2. Sentence 2 ____________ ____________ ____________

3. Sentence 3 ____________ ____________ ____________

B. Foods can be green, red, or orange.

1. Draw a picture of a food for each color.

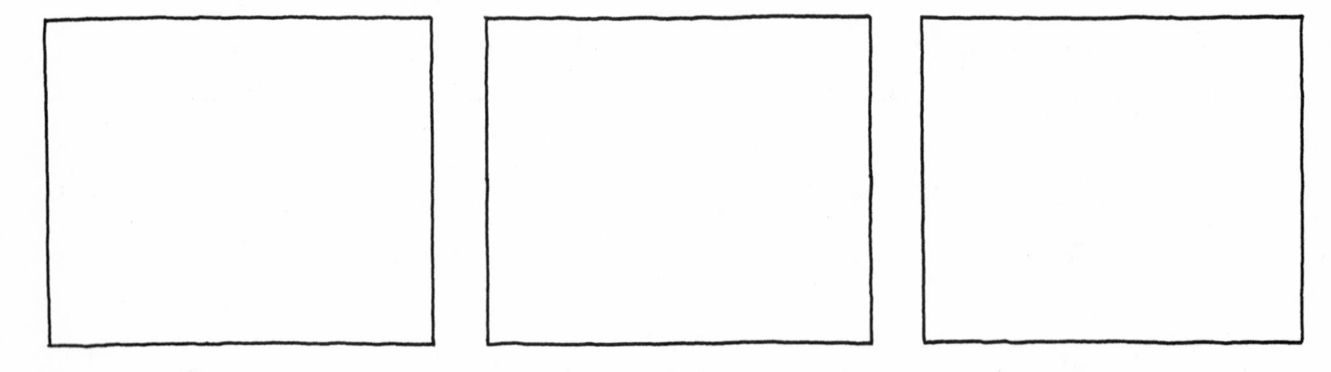

green red orange

2. Write a sentence. List the foods you drew.

____

WHILE YOU READ

Tip Look for commas between words in a list. Commas help you find the things in the list.

There are different kinds of animals. They are pets, wild animals, and farm animals.

Dogs, cats, and some birds are pet animals. Some people keep animals like turtles and mice as pets. But they are really wild animals.

Most wild animals do not make good pets. You should not keep a raccoon, deer, or bear as a pet. These animals live best in the wild.

Cows, goats, pigs, and sheep are farm animals. People raise these animals to help us live. We get things like milk, meat, and wool from farm animals.

AFTER YOU READ

A. Fill in the circle for the answer.

1. The story tells about ______ kinds of animals.

○ three ○ four ○ five

2. Which is the best name for the story?

○ "Wild Animals" ○ "Farm Life" ○ "Kinds of Animals"

3. What kind of animal is a deer?

○ pet ○ farm ○ wild

B. Find a picture of an animal. Write a sentence listing three or four things about the animal, such as, "The bear is big, brown, and furry."

YOU KNOW

- A sentence that shows surprise or strong feeling ends with this mark (!).
- These marks (" ") are used around the exact words a speaker says.
- A comma (,) is used between each word in a list.

A. Read each sentence. Put a ✓ in front of the sentence if it shows surprise or strong feeling.

1. _____ It was a very cold day.

2. _____ All of a sudden it began to snow!

3. _____ Where could Mouse go?

4. _____ Then Mouse saw a big mitten!

B. Underline the exact words each animal said.

1. "That mitten looks warm," said Mouse.

2. Mouse said, "This will be a good home."

3. Bird asked, "May I come in, too?"

4. "Let me in the mitten!" shouted Squirrel.

C. Read each sentence. Underline the sentence if it has words in a list.

1. Mouse, Bird, and Squirrel were in the mitten.

2. The mitten was soft, warm, and crowded.

3. The three animals began to sing a song.

4. They sang fast, loud, and funny songs.

 Review—exclamation mark, quotation marks, commas; using punctuation marks to understand exclamatory sentences, sentences with quotation marks, and sentences with commas in a series

USING WHAT YOU KNOW

Mouse, Bird, and Squirrel were singing in the mitten. Then Rabbit came along. "It is so cold out here!" Rabbit said. "May I come in with you?"

"No room!" said Mouse, Bird, and Squirrel.

But Rabbit pushed herself into the mitten anyway. Mouse, Bird, and Squirrel moved over to make room for Rabbit.

Along came Raccoon. "I'm very cold!" said Raccoon. "May I come in?"

"Too tight!" said Mouse, Bird, Squirrel, and Rabbit.

But Raccoon got into the mitten anyway.

1. Look at the picture. Put a ✓ in front of what the animals in the mitten said.

____ "I'm very cold!"

____ "No room!"

____ "Too tight!"

____ "May I come in?"

2. Underline each sentence in part 1 that was said with strong feeling.

3. Look at the story. Write the names of the animals that were in the mitten first.

________________ ________________ ________________

WHILE YOU READ

Tip Look at the marks at the beginning and the end of a sentence. Also look for commas between words in a list. These marks will help you understand what you read.

Along came Bear. "What a warm mitten!" said Bear. "It is very cold out. May I join you?"

"No more room!" shouted Mouse, Bird, Squirrel, Rabbit, and Raccoon.

Bear growled, "You can make some room for me!" So the animals let Bear in.

A tiny fly came along next. "I am so cold!" Fly said. "Please let me in." They let Fly in because he was so little.

But that was too much for the mitten. It ripped open. All the animals were cold again!

AFTER YOU READ

A. Fill in the circle for the answer.

1. What did the animals say to Bear?

○ "Let me in." ○ "No more room!" ○ "May I join you?"

2. The mitten ripped open because it was too

○ full ○ soft ○ warm

3. How many animals were cold at the end?

○ five ○ six ○ seven

B. Read the story on pages 119 and 120 to a friend. The marks in the sentences help you know how to read them.

Lesson 10 CUMULATIVE REVIEW

Have you ever waved good-by? Have you ever pointed with your finger to show where something is? If you have, you have talked with your hands.

People who cannot hear often talk with their hands. They use many different hand signs. There are signs for letters, numbers, words, and ideas. A person can put together these signs to say just about anything he or she wants to say.

1. To say good-by, you can–
   - ○ point
   - ○ wave
   - ○ count

2. How can people who cannot hear say things?
   - ○ by reading letters
   - ○ by waving their hands
   - ○ by using hand signs

3. A good name for the story is–
   - ○ "People Who Hear"
   - ○ "Talking With Your Hands"
   - ○ "Number Signs"

Carmel got a new puppy. She wanted to teach it to be a good dog. But Carmel cannot hear, so she could not speak to her puppy. She used hand signs instead.

The first sign the puppy learned was the sign for <u>dog</u>. First Carmel patted herself on the leg. Then she snapped her fingers. When the puppy saw Carmel do these things, the puppy knew Carmel was talking to it.

4. What was the first step in the sign for <u>dog</u>?
   - ○ snap your fingers
   - ○ say the word <u>dog</u>
   - ○ pat your leg

5. Carmel used hand signs to–
   - ○ talk to her puppy
   - ○ understand her puppy
   - ○ see her puppy

6. The puppy knew Carmel was talking to it when she–
   - ○ opened her mouth
   - ○ made the sign for <u>dog</u>
   - ○ came into the room

DEAF DONALD

Deaf Donald met Talkie Sue

But   was all he could do.

And Sue said, "Donald, I sure do like you."

But   was all he could do.

And Sue asked Donald, "Do you like me too?"

But   was all he could do.

"Good-bye then, Donald, I'm leaving you."

But   was all he did do.

And she left forever so she never knew

That   means I love you.

Shel Silverstein

7. What did Sue say to Donald?
- ○ "I sure do like you."
- ○ "Where are you?"
- ○ "I am moving away."

8. Donald made hand signs because he–
- ○ did not want to talk
- ○ could not hear
- ○ was afraid of Sue

9. Sue wanted Donald to–
- ○ teach her hand signs
- ○ go away
- ○ talk to her

10. Sue left because Donald–
- ○ did not like her
- ○ was mean to her
- ○ did not speak to her

11. What was Donald saying?
- ○ "I see you."
- ○ "I love you."
- ○ "I miss you."

12. If Sue knew what Donald was saying, she would have–
- ○ stayed
- ○ jumped up
- ○ gone away

People use their bodies to give information. They nod to say "yes." They shake their heads to say "no." They lift their shoulders to say "I don't know." These actions are called body language.

Smiles and frowns are body language, too. Other people know what you mean when you do these things.

Do you yawn when you are tired? Do you put a finger over your mouth when you want someone to be quiet? You are using body language!

Body language is used all the time. Just look around you.

You can see people using body language in the street. A crossing guard uses hand signs to tell drivers and other people when to stop and go. A person on a bike puts out an arm to show a right or left turn.

You can see people using body language in games, too. In baseball, arms spread out can mean a player is safe. But a thumb pointed over a shoulder says, "You're out!"

13. Body language is using your body to–
- ○ make noise
- ○ give information
- ○ know what people mean

14. What are you telling other people when you yawn?
- ○ I'm hungry.
- ○ I'm proud.
- ○ I'm tired.

15. When you watch a baseball game, body language can tell you a player is–
- ○ fast
- ○ safe
- ○ good

16. From the story, you know that body language can–
- ○ teach you how to ride a bike
- ○ make you lose a game
- ○ help you stay safe in the street

DETAILS / REMEMBERING INFORMATION

- You can get information from things you read.

Read the story.

A camel can live in a place where food is hard to find. How does it do this?

The hump of a camel is really a large lump of fat. When a camel cannot find food, it uses the fat in its hump like food. The hump becomes smaller when the camel goes for a long time without real food. But when the camel gets more food, the hump grows big again.

Read the question. Find the answer in the story. Write the answer.

1. Where can a camel live? ____________________

____

2. What is the hump of a camel? ____________________
3. When food is hard to find, what does a camel use instead? ____________________
4. What happens to the hump after a long time without food? ____________________
5. What happens to the hump when the camel gets more food? ____________________

USING WHAT YOU KNOW

A camel lives in a sandy place. Special parts of its body help it live there.

A camel walks and runs on sand. Its feet are wide with soft pads. Its feet do not sink into the sand when the camel takes steps.

Sometimes there is a storm. Sand blows all around. But a camel is not hurt by the sand. Its eyes have two rows of lashes that keep out sand. Its ears are covered with hair that helps keep out sand. Its nose has very thin openings that can be closed. Sand cannot go up its nose when these openings are closed.

As you read, try to remember the information in the story. Remembering this information helps you understand the story.

1. What special parts of a camel are named in the story? Write them here.

____________ ____________ ____________ ____________

2. Look at the picture. Circle each part of the camel that helps it live in a sandy place.

WHILE YOU READ

As you read, try to remember the information in the story. Remembering information will help you better understand what you read.

In 1857, the United States Army bought 75 camels. The camels were very helpful. They carried heavy things across the land, rivers, and mountains in New Mexico and California.

Many people in this country did not like the camels. The camels looked strange to them. The camels frightened their horses and mules.

In 1864, the army sold all its camels. Some camels were sold to carry mail. Some camels went to circuses. And some were set free to live in the sandy places they liked best.

AFTER YOU READ

A. Fill in the circle for the answer.

1. Camels helped the army by

○ looking strange ○ carrying things ○ being free

2. People did not like camels because they

○ carried mail ○ liked sand ○ scared animals

3. The story is mostly about camels in the

○ circus ○ United States ○ mountains

B. Some camels have one hump. Some have two humps. Look at the pictures on pages 124 and 125. Try to draw a camel with two humps.

Lesson 2 DETAILS / REMEMBERING IMPORTANT INFORMATION

YOU KNOW

- You should try to remember the information in what you read.

Read the story.

Jana cut shapes in a piece of cardboard. She put the cardboard on top of a piece of paper. Then she got a jar of paint and a brush. She brushed the paint over the shapes in the cardboard. The paint went through the shapes and made a picture on the paper. Jana carefully lifted up the cardboard. Then she hung up her picture to dry.

Read the sentence. Put a ✓ in front of the sentence if it tells information from the story.

1. _____ Jana cut shapes in some cardboard.

2. _____ The cardboard was brown.

3. _____ Jana put the cardboard on a piece of paper.

4. _____ Jana brushed paint over the shapes.

5. _____ Some paint splashed on the floor.

6. _____ The paint went through the shapes.

7. _____ Jana lifted up the cardboard.

8. _____ Jana hung up the picture to dry.

9. _____ It took three hours for the paint to dry.

USING WHAT YOU KNOW

1. Jana was in the second grade. 2. She wanted to make pictures for her class. 3. She used her piece of cardboard to make a picture for each person in her class.

Look at the story. Sentences 2 and 3 tell information that is important to remember if you want to understand the story. The information in sentence 1 is not as important because it does not help you understand the story. When you read, decide which information is important. Then try to remember that information.

A. Read the next part of the story. Decide which information is important. Try to remember it.

The pictures were very pretty. Jana wrote a name on each one. Then she packed the pictures in a box and tied some string around it. She put the box near the door so she would not forget to take it to school.

B. Read the sentence. Underline the sentence if it tells information that helps you understand the story.

1. The pictures were very pretty.
2. Jana wrote a name on each picture.
3. Jana packed the pictures in a box.
4. Jana tied string around the box.
5. Jana put the box near the door.

WHILE YOU READ

When you read, decide which information is important and try to remember it. Doing this will help you understand the story.

Jana took the box of pictures to school. She got there early. She started putting a picture on each desk. Soon all the pictures were gone. Jana looked at the desks. There was a picture on every desk but one. Jana was worried. "Did I forget someone?" she wondered.

Jana's friends came into the room. They found their pictures. Everyone was there. Everyone had a picture. Then Jana knew who sat at the desk without a picture. She did!

AFTER YOU READ

A. Fill in the circle for the answer.

1. How many desks did not have a picture?
○ one ○ two ○ many

2. Jana forgot to bring a picture for
○ her sister ○ a friend ○ herself

3. Jana got to school early to
○ make a picture ○ clean her desk ○ surprise her friends

4. Which word tells about Jana?
○ tall ○ nice ○ sad

B. Make a picture like Jana's. The story on page 127 tells you how.

Details; distinguishing between important and unimportant details; using important details to understand selections

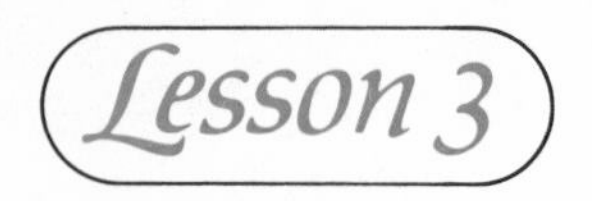

SEQUENCE / REMEMBERING WHEN THINGS HAPPEN

YOU KNOW

- Things happen in a certain order in a story.
- Words like first, next, and last can tell when things happen.

Read the story.

The spaceship stands on its pad. First there is a roaring noise that gets louder and louder. Next, fire and smoke pour out of the bottom of the spaceship. At last the spaceship lifts off, trailing a tail of fire behind it.

A. Read the sentence. Write **first, next,** or **last** to show when things happen.

1. Fire and smoke come from the spaceship. ____________

2. The spaceship lifts off. ____________

3. There is a loud roaring noise. ____________

B. Read the word. Draw a line to the picture that goes with the word.

1. first

2. next

3. last

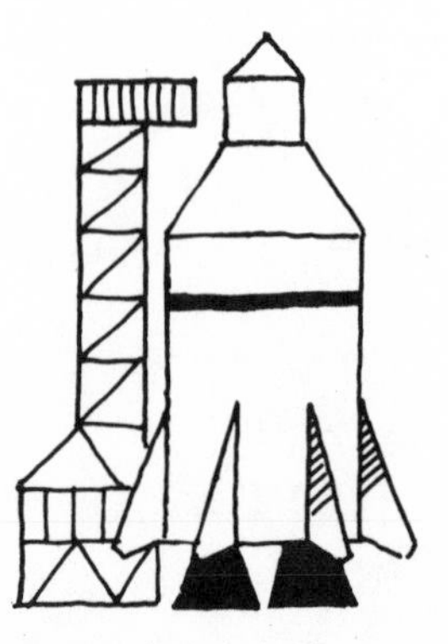

 Sequence; recognizing clue words that indicate sequence; using sequence clue words to understand selections

USING WHAT YOU KNOW

The United States has sent spaceships carrying many different things into space. The first things sent up were machines. Then two monkeys were sent into space. Later a chimp was sent up in a spaceship. After that, a man went into space. He stayed there for just 15 minutes. Now many people can go into space together. They can stay there for many days.

The underlined words in the story help you remember the order in which things happened. Remembering the order in which things happened helps you understand the story.

1. Look at the pictures. Write **1, 2, 3, 4,** or **5** in the box to show the order in which things happened in the story.

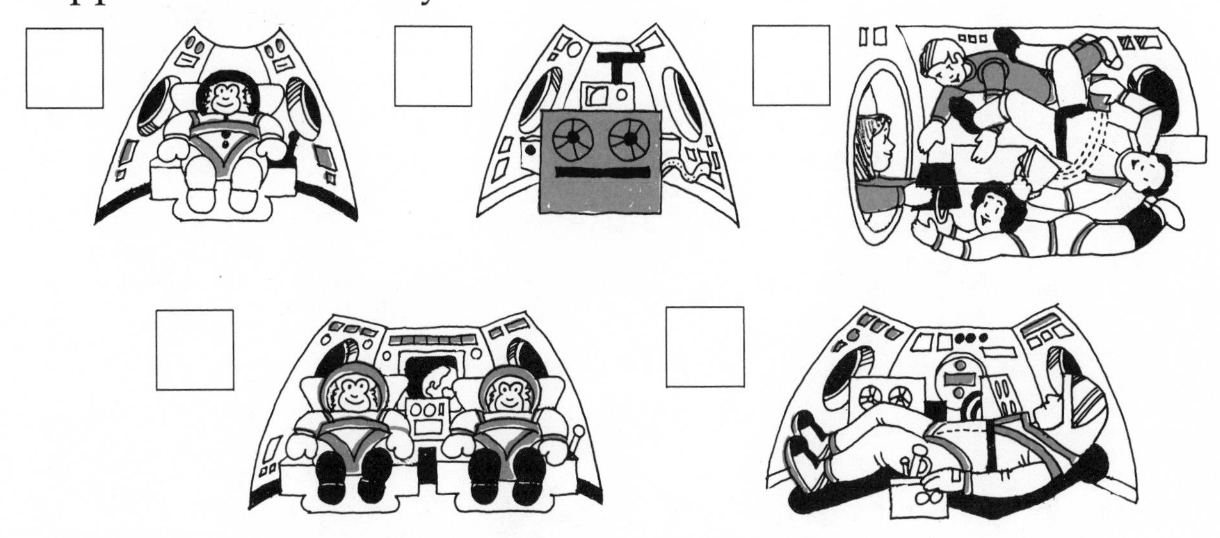

2. What cannot travel into space now? Circle the answer.   animals   people   buildings

WHILE YOU READ

Look for words like first and then to help you remember when things happen in the story. If you remember when things happen, you will better understand what you read.

Oscar was on his first trip into space. He couldn't wait to explore the spaceship.

"Be careful, Oscar," his mother said. "You haven't learned how to move in space yet."

First Oscar let go of the wall strap. Then he pushed off. He shot across the ship. The next thing he knew, he had bounced off the wall. Then he rolled over and over in the air. Finally he grabbed the wall strap again.

"Whew!" said Oscar. "I guess I do have a few things to learn about moving in space!"

AFTER YOU READ

A. Fill in the circle for the answer.

1. The first thing Oscar did was

○ grab the strap ○ let go ○ move the ship

2. After Oscar bounced off the wall, he

○ rolled over ○ held on ○ pushed off

3. What was Oscar trying to do?

○ scare his mother ○ play ball ○ move in space

B. Pretend you are on the spaceship, too. Draw what you saw when you explored the ship.

 Sequence; recognizing clue words that indicate sequence; using sequence clue words to understand selections

YOU KNOW

- You should try to remember the information in what you read.
- Words like first, next, and last can tell when things happen in a story.

Read the story.

The bell rings in the firehouse. This means there is a fire. The first thing the fire fighters do is grab their hats, coats, and boots. Next, they jump onto their trucks. Last, the fire trucks race off to the fire.

A. Read the sentence. Put a ✓ in front of the sentence if it tells information from the story.

1. _____ The bell rings in the firehouse.
2. _____ The bell rings for a long time.
3. _____ The fire fighters jump onto their trucks.
4. _____ There are six fire fighters on each truck.
5. _____ The fire trucks race off to the fire.

B. Read the sentence. Write **first, next,** or **last** to show when things happen.

1. The fire trucks race to the fire. ____________
2. The fire fighters grab their clothes. ____________
3. The fire fighters jump onto their trucks. ____________

USING WHAT YOU KNOW

The fire trucks reach the burning building. First the fire fighters jump off the trucks. Next, some of them pull hoses from the trucks. At the same time, other fire fighters make sure no one is trapped inside the building. Then they put out the fire. After the fire is out, the fire fighters make sure it cannot start burning again. Finally, the fire trucks go back to the firehouse.

A. Read the sentence. Write **1, 2, 3, 4,** or **5** on the line to show the order in which things happen in the story.

_____ Some fire fighters pull hoses from the trucks.

_____ The fire trucks go back to the firehouse.

_____ The fire fighters make sure the fire cannot start again.

_____ The fire fighters get off the trucks.

_____ The fire fighters put out the fire.

B. Underline each sentence in part A that tells information that helps you understand the story.

C. Write two important things fire fighters do.

1. ______________________________

2. ______________________________

 Review—details, sequence; recognizing and using important details and sequence clue words to understand selections

WHILE YOU READ

Tip When you read the story, decide which information is important and try to remember it. Also look for words that help you remember when things happen. These things will help you understand what you read.

Beth's class was visiting a firehouse. She saw a tall pole in the room with the fire trucks.

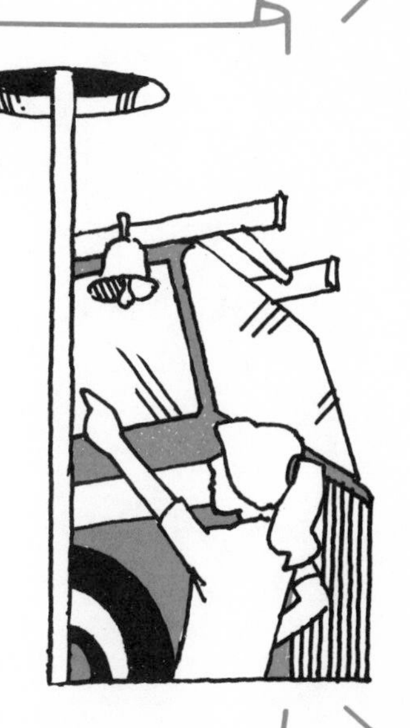

"What is the pole for?" Beth asked.

A loud bell rang before anyone could answer her. Then a fire fighter came sliding down the pole. He ran to a truck after he reached the ground. One after the other, the fire fighters slid down the pole and ran to the trucks.

"Now I know what the pole is for!" said Beth.

AFTER YOU READ

A. Fill in the circle for the answer.

1. What did Beth see in the fire truck room?

○ a slide ○ stairs ○ a pole

2. The fire fighters ran to the trucks

○ before they slid down the pole
○ after they reached the ground
○ before the bell rang

3. The fire fighters used the pole to

○ hold their coats ○ get down fast ○ fix the trucks

B. You can make a new word, like firefly, by adding a word to fire. Write five new words with fire.

Lesson 5 STORIES / FINDING THE MAIN IDEA SENTENCE

YOU KNOW

- A group of sentences can tell about the same idea.

Read the story. All the sentences tell about a baby frog.

> A baby frog is like a little fish. It can breathe underwater. It has a long tail to help it swim. It swims around in the water looking for food.

Read each story. All the sentences but one are about the same idea. Cross out the sentence that does not belong.

1. Frogs can see well. This helps them catch food. They push their eyes out so they can see in all directions. Frogs can hear, too.

2. Frogs eat many different things. Some frogs hunt for food. Most of the time frogs eat insects. Sometimes they eat worms and spiders. Big frogs may eat smaller frogs!

3. Some frogs may live for many years. Other animals eat young frogs. Raccoons like to eat frogs. So do snakes, turtles, and fish.

4. A grown-up frog has four legs. It uses its back legs for jumping and swimming. Its front legs help it sit up. Some frogs sit on trees.

USING WHAT YOU KNOW

A baby frog goes through many changes to become a grown-up frog. Its tail gets smaller and back legs start to grow. Then front legs start to grow. At the same time, the baby frog changes inside. The changes inside let the frog breathe air and eat small animals.

The main idea of a story is what the story is mostly about. A story may begin or end with a sentence that tells the main idea. To find the main idea sentence, look for the sentence that tells what the whole story is about.

1. In the story at the top, underline the sentence that tells the main idea.

2. Look at each picture. Write **baby** or **grown-up.**

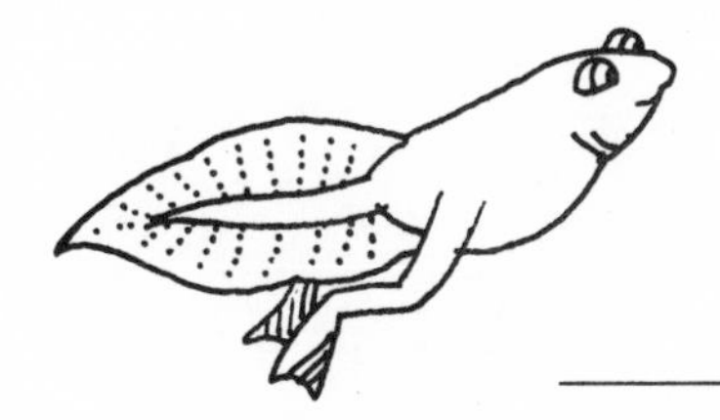 ______________

 ______________

3. Read the story below. Underline the sentence that tells the main idea.

   Most frogs are brown or green. Some frogs are both brown and green. Other frogs have bright orange marks on their skin. Frogs can be different colors.

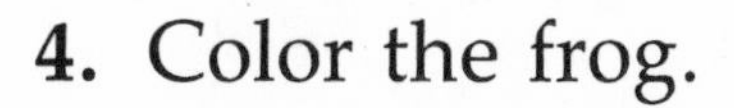

4. Color the frog.

WHILE YOU READ

Tip As you read, look for the main idea sentence. It will tell you what the whole story is about.

Fred Frog met Fran Frog near the pond.

"Hi," said Fran. "Look at my new legs. Having legs is so much fun!"

"My legs just grew, too," said Fred. "I like my legs, but I'm going to miss my tail."

"Me, too," said Fran. "A tail made it so easy to swim."

"Gee," said Fred. "We seem to be a lot alike. What is your favorite food?"

"Flies," said Fran. "I just love flies!"

"Me, too!" cried Fred. "Hey, we really are very much alike, aren't we?"

AFTER YOU READ

A. Fill in the circle for the answer.

1. Fran and Fred both like to

○ eat flies ○ jump ○ turn green

2. The main idea sentence of the story is the

○ first sentence ○ fifth sentence ○ last sentence

3. What is the story mostly about?

○ how Fran and Fred grew legs

○ how Fran and Fred are alike

○ how Fran and Fred lost their tails

B. After school, play leapfrog with your friends.

Lesson 6 MAIN IDEA / WHAT A STORY IS ABOUT

YOU KNOW

- The main idea of a story is what the story is mostly about.
- A story may begin or end with a sentence that tells the main idea.

Read the story. Look for the main idea sentence.

Kites have helped people in many ways. They have been used to help people build bridges and airplanes. They have helped people find out what the weather will be like. They have also been used to help people take pictures from up in the air. Kites have also just helped people have fun!

1. In the story above, underline the main idea sentence.

2. Read the story below. Underline the main idea sentence.

Once a kite is in the air, try moving the string different ways. Move the string left, right, up, and down. Watch what happens as you move the string. Then think about where you want the kite to go. Move the string so the kite goes that way. You can learn to make the kite go wherever you want it to go.

3. Finish the sentence.

Both stories on this page are about ________________.

USING WHAT YOU KNOW

There are small light kites that can fly where there is very little wind. There are strong kites that can pull hard and lift heavy things. There are round and square kites. There are kites that look like boxes and kites that look like animals. There are even dragon kites that are made of many round kites held together by string.

Sometimes a story does not have a sentence that tells the main idea. Then you should think of the one important idea all the sentences tell about. Knowing the important idea helps you understand the story.

1. Underline the sentence that tells the main idea of the story.

   There are kites that look like dragons.
   There are many kinds of kites.
   Kites can lift heavy things.

2. Six words from the story that tell about kites are hidden in the puzzle. Find the words. Look across and down. Circle each word.

s	m	a	l	l	a	s
t	r	o	r	x	n	q
r	o	u	n	d	i	u
o	l	l	b	s	m	a
n	q	m	o	d	a	r
g	d	n	x	l	l	e

WHILE YOU READ

Think of the one important idea all the sentences in the story tell about. Knowing this idea will help you understand the story.

"Our kite won't fly if there is not enough wind," Erica told her brother, Sean. "And too much wind will hurt the kite."

"How can we tell when the wind is right?" asked Sean.

"Look at the trees," Erica answered. "The wind is right when the leaves are moving but the branches are not."

Sean looked at the trees.

"Is the wind right now?" asked Erica.

"Yes!" said Sean. "Let's go."

AFTER YOU READ

A. Fill in the circle for the answer.

1. What is the main idea of the story?

○ You need the right kind of wind to fly a kite.
○ You cannot fly a kite on a windy day.
○ The leaves on tree branches move in the wind.

2. If there is too much wind, a kite may

○ not move ○ break ○ run away

3. What will Erica and Sean do next?

○ go home ○ watch the trees ○ fly their kite

B. Draw a picture of a kite you would like to fly.

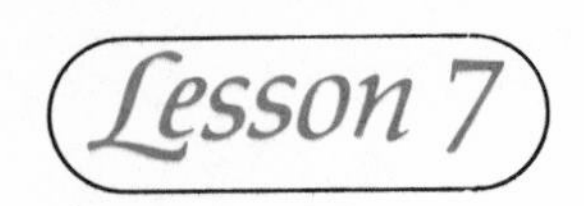

MAIN IDEA / REMEMBERING WHAT A STORY IS ABOUT

- A story does not always have a sentence that tells the main idea.

Read each story. Think of the one important idea all the sentences tell about.

1. President Jimmy Carter made a tree house for his daughter Amy. The tree house was near the White House, which is the place a President and his family live. The tree house looked like a big box on poles. Amy liked to sit in the tree house and read.

2. If you want to build a tree house, look for a big tree with strong branches. Branches in the shape of the letter V are best. They will hold the house up well. Also look for a spot that is not too high up. It will be easier to climb up to and down from your house if it is closer to the ground.

1. Put a ✓ in front of the sentence that tells the main idea of story 1.

_____ The tree house looked like a box on poles.
_____ There was a tree house near the White House.
_____ Amy liked to read in the tree house.

2. Put a ✓ in front of the sentence that tells the main idea of story 2.

_____ A tree with strong branches is the best kind.
_____ A tree house should not be too high up.
_____ You should find a good spot for a tree house.

USING WHAT YOU KNOW

A tree house is a different kind of place. You can be quiet or noisy there. You can be all by yourself, or you can be with your friends. You can tell a tree house your secrets, and it won't tell them to anyone!

You feel something special when you are in a tree house. When the wind blows, the tree moves. The tree house moves, too. You feel that you are part of the tree.

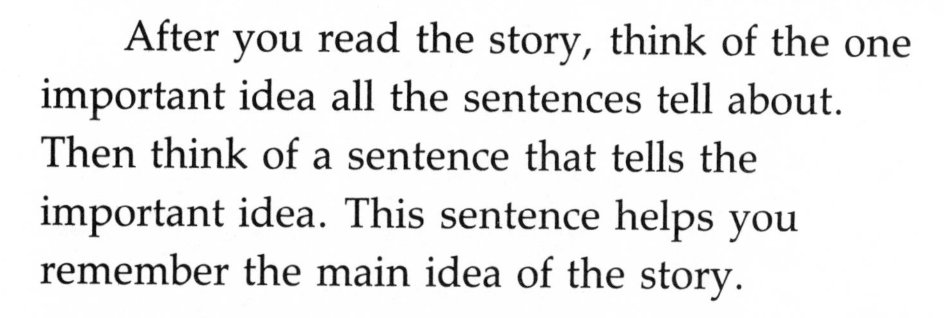

After you read the story, think of the one important idea all the sentences tell about. Then think of a sentence that tells the important idea. This sentence helps you remember the main idea of the story.

A. 1. What one important idea do all the sentences tell about? Underline the answer.

how to live in a tree house

how a tree house is special

how a tree house moves

2. Write a sentence that tells the main idea of the story.

____

B. Write what you would do in a tree house.

____

WHILE YOU READ

Tip Think of a sentence that tells the one important idea in the poem. This sentence will help you remember the main idea of the poem.

TREE HOUSE

A tree house, a free house,
A secret you and me house,
A high up in the leafy branches
Cozy as can be house.

A street house, a neat house,
Be sure and wipe your feet house
Is not my kind of house at all—
Let's go live in a tree house.

Shel Silverstein

AFTER YOU READ

A. 1. Fill in the circle for the answer. The person in the poem likes a tree house

- ○ less than a neat house
- ○ better than a street house
- ○ instead of a high house

2. Write a sentence that tells the main idea of the poem.

____

B. Draw a picture of your favorite kind of house.

Lesson 8 **REVIEW**

YOU KNOW

- The main idea of a story is what the story is mostly about.
- A story may or may not begin or end with a sentence that tells the main idea.

1. Read the story. Underline the main idea sentence.

Long ago, it is said, the sun moved across the sky very quickly. The days were short. There wasn't much sunlight. The days were cold, too. It was like winter all the time.

2. Read the story below.

A man named Maui got a very long rope. He tied it into a big circle at one end. As the sun rose, Maui threw his rope and caught the sun. The sun begged Maui to let it go.

"I will let you go if you promise to move more slowly," Maui said to the sun.

"I like to go fast," said the sun. "Let me go fast some of the time, and then I will go slowly some of the time."

"Very well," said Maui.

3. Put a ✓ in front of the sentence that tells the main idea of the story in part 2.

_____ The sun liked to go fast.

_____ Maui made the sun move more slowly.

_____ The days were long and warm in summer.

USING WHAT YOU KNOW

Long ago, it is told, people did not know how to make fire. Only the mud hens knew how. Maui wanted to get some fire for his people. But each time he came near the hens, they scratched out the fire.

One day Maui caught a small mud hen. "Where does the fire come from?" he asked.

"It comes from that plant," the hen said.

Maui rubbed the plant, but no fire came from it. He asked the hen again.

"It comes from that tree," the hen said.

Maui rubbed the tree, but no fire came from it. So he asked the hen again.

Finally the hen told Maui the secret. Maui then took the fire back to his people.

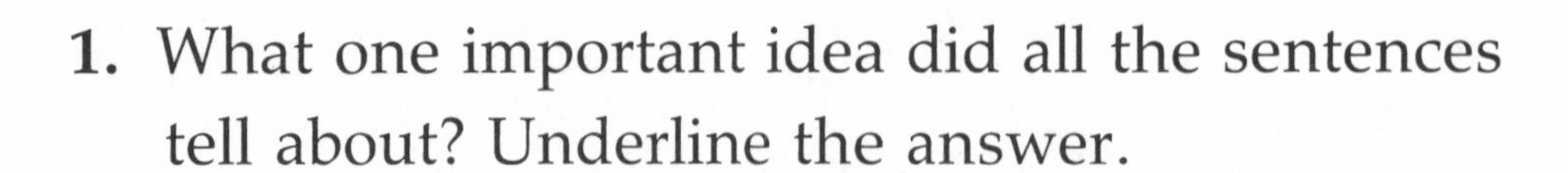

1. What one important idea did all the sentences tell about? Underline the answer.

   how Maui rubbed plants and trees

   how the mud hens scratched out fires

   how Maui learned to make fire

2. Write a sentence that tells the main idea of the story.

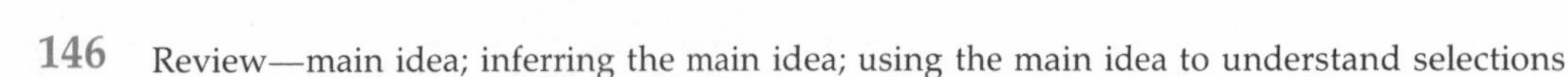

WHILE YOU READ

Tip As you read, think of the one important idea all the sentences tell about. This will help you remember the main idea of the story.

Hawaii has eight big islands. The Wise One said to Maui, "The islands will move together if you catch the magic fish. But you must not look at the fish until it is on land."

Maui and his brother went fishing. They caught the magic fish. As they dragged the fish behind their boat, the islands started to move together.

"Look!" cried Maui's brother. As he turned around to speak to Maui, the hook slipped from the fish's mouth. The fish swam away and the islands moved apart.

AFTER YOU READ

A. Fill in the circle for the answer.

1. The islands moved apart because Maui's brother

○ ate the fish ○ went fishing ○ lost the fish

2. Maui and his brother tried to

○ move the islands ○ be very wise ○ make more islands

3. Write a sentence that tells the main idea of the story.

____

B. Draw a picture to go with the story.

Lesson 9 CAUSE AND EFFECT / WHY THINGS HAPPEN

YOU KNOW

- One thing can make another thing happen.
- The words because and so can be used in a sentence to tell why something happens.

Read the story.

Hiroshi woke up and looked at the clock. "Oh, no!" he cried. "I'm late for school!" Hiroshi did not wait for breakfast because he was late. He left right away so he would not miss the school bus.

Hiroshi thought he had missed the bus because no one was at the stop. He ran all the way to school so he would get there on time.

Write the answer.

1. Why didn't Hiroshi wait for breakfast?

____

2. Why did Hiroshi leave right away?

____

3. Why did Hiroshi think he had missed the bus?

____

4. Why did Hiroshi run all the way to school?

____

 Cause and effect; recognizing cause-and-effect relationships; understanding why things in a selection happen

USING WHAT YOU KNOW

At last Hiroshi got to school. He was out of breath from running. He stopped to rest. Then he looked around.

Something was wrong. The schoolyard was empty. The classroom windows were empty. No one was around. Hiroshi grew worried. He went to the door and tried to open it, but the door was locked. Hiroshi couldn't get into school!

Sometimes a story does not use the words because and so to tell why things happened. But you can still find out why something happened if you think about what happened first. What happened first tells you why something else happened. When you know why things happened, you understand the story better.

A. Read the sentence. Draw a line to the word or words that tell why it happened.

1. Hiroshi was out of breath.	door was locked
2. Hiroshi stopped to rest.	no one was around
3. Hiroshi got worried.	out of breath
4. Hiroshi couldn't get into school.	running

B. Write why you think no one was at school.

____

WHILE YOU READ

To find out why something happens, think about what happens first. Knowing why things happen will help you understand the story.

For a minute Hiroshi didn't understand why the school door was locked. Then he remembered. It was Saturday! Of course no one was at school!

Hiroshi walked back home slowly. He was tired from the long run to school.

"Today didn't start out very well," Hiroshi said to himself. "I think I'll go back to bed and start the day over again."

AFTER YOU READ

A. Fill in the circle for the answer.

1. No one was at school because it was

○ summer ○ nighttime ○ Saturday

2. Why did Hiroshi walk home slowly?

○ He was happy.
○ He was tired.
○ He was sick.

3. If he can start the day over, Hiroshi hopes the day will be

○ longer ○ better ○ sunny

B. On which days do you go to school? List the seven days of the week. Write **school** or **no school** after each day.

 Cause and effect; recognizing cause-and-effect relationships; understanding why things in a selection happen

Lesson 10 DRAWING CONCLUSIONS / ANSWERING RIDDLES

YOU KNOW

- What a writer tells helps you understand things about a story.

Read the story.

Melba and Leon were hunting all over the room. Melba was looking for her mitt. Leon was looking for his bat. At last they found their things. They were ready to go to the ball field.

"Let's hurry!" said Melba. "We should have left a long time ago. Everyone will be there waiting for us."

Put a ✓ in front of the answer.

1. First the writer tells you Melba and Leon were looking for a mitt and a bat. Then the writer tells you they were going to the ball field. These two things help you know that

_____ Melba and Leon were the same age

_____ Melba and Leon were going to play ball

2. Next the writer tells you Melba and Leon should have left a long time ago. This helps you know that

_____ Melba and Leon were late

_____ Melba and Leon had many friends

USING WHAT YOU KNOW

I have four wheels. You wear me on your feet. My wheels roll along the ground. I help you move quickly. What am I?

roller skates

The writer does not tell you the answer to the riddle above. But the underlined words are clues that help you know what the riddle is about. They help you answer the riddle. Turn your book upside down to see if your answer is right.

Read each riddle. Write the answer. After you answer riddle 3, turn your book upside down to see if your answers are right.

1. I am made out of cloth or plastic. I have a tail and a long string. I can fly very high when there is a good wind. You must hold my string or I will fly away. What am I? ____________

2. I have two big wheels, one behind the other. I have two handles. You sit on me and hold my handles. You move your feet to make me go. What am I? ____________

3. I am long and thin. You hold me by my ends. You make me go over your head. Then you make me go under your feet. You jump over me again and again. What am I? ____________

1. kite 2. bike 3. jump rope

WHILE YOU READ

Tip Look for the clue words in each riddle. The clue words will help you find the answer to the riddle.

1. I have a flat top and two curved pieces below. On a snowy day you take me up a hill. Then you sit on me and down the hill we go. If you want to go down again, you have to take me back up the hill. What am I?

2. I have a small flat seat and a chain on each side. You sit on me and hold my chains. Back and forth we go, higher and higher. When we stop, we are back where we started. What am I?

AFTER YOU READ

A. Fill in the circle for the answer.

1. What is the answer to riddle 1?

○ a table ○ a sled ○ a snowball

2. What is the answer to riddle 2?

○ a swing ○ a chair ○ a horse

3. Both riddles are about things you can

○ eat with ○ play ○ ride on

B. Pick something you like to play with or eat. Write a riddle about it. End your riddle with the words, "What am I?" Read your riddle to a friend. Did your friend guess the answer?

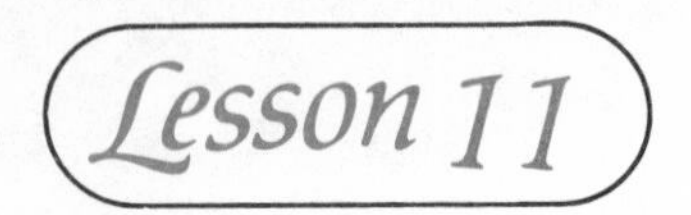

DRAWING CONCLUSIONS / STORY SENSE

YOU KNOW

- A writer does not always tell you everything you need to know.

Read the story.

"Is everyone coming to Racing Day tomorrow?" Ms. Waters asked her class on the last day of the week.

"Yes," answered the class.

"Remember, not everyone can win," said Ms. Waters. "But everyone can have fun. Let's make a list of the races you will be in."

After you read the story you know that Ms. Waters is a teacher and that it was Friday. But the writer did not tell you these things.

Read the sentences. Put a ✓ in front of the answer that you know but the writer didn't tell you.

1. Ms. Waters called on Nancy. "I'm going to be in the Two-Wheel Race," Nancy said.

_____ Nancy will be in a running race.
_____ Nancy will be in a bike race.
_____ Nancy will be in a swimming race.

2. Ricky would not say which race he will be in.

_____ Ricky had a secret plan.
_____ Ricky did not want to be in a race.
_____ Ricky will be in three races.

USING WHAT YOU KNOW

It was Racing Day. Everyone came to school early. The children laughed and talked about the races.

A sign told where each race would be. One sign said, "Four-Wheel Race." Another sign said, "Eight-Wheel Race." Nancy wheeled her bike toward the sign that said, "Two-Wheel Race." She waved to Rita, who was carrying her roller skates.

"Have you seen Ricky?" Nancy asked.

"No, I haven't seen him," answered Rita.

Think about the things the writer told you in the story. Use those things to find out what the writer did not tell you. What you find out should make sense because of what you read in the story.

Circle the answer. Write it on the line in the school.

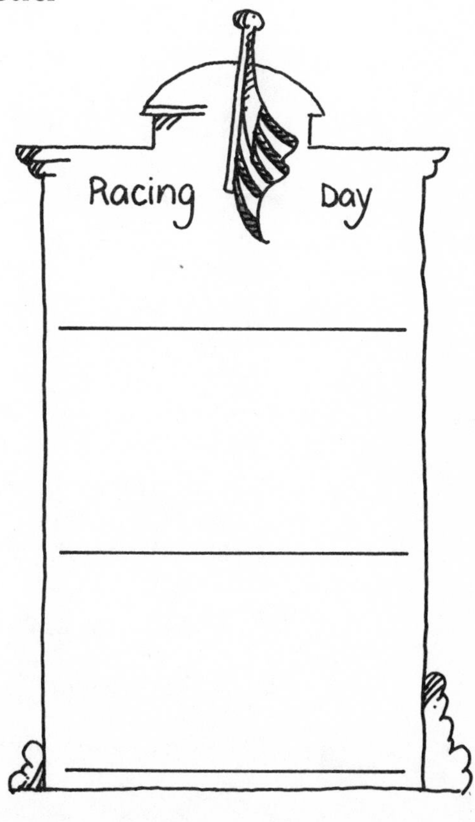

1. The children at school were
   lost happy sad

2. To be in a race, you had to be on something with
   wheels feet signs

3. Rita will be in a race for ______ wheels.
   two five eight

WHILE YOU READ

Tip Use what the writer tells to find out what the writer does not tell. What you find out should agree with what you read in the story.

There wasn't a cloud in the sky. The air was warm. It was a great day for racing.

Nancy and Rita kept thinking about Ricky. They wondered where he was. They wanted to know what he was going to do.

Then Rita saw Ricky. "Look at Ricky!" she shouted in a loud voice.

Everyone looked. Ricky was on a bike with just one wheel!

"Ricky will win his race," said Nancy. "He is the only one here on just one wheel!"

AFTER YOU READ

A. Fill in the circle for the answer.

1. What kind of day was it?

○ sunny ○ rainy ○ cloudy

2. When Rita saw Ricky, she was

○ afraid ○ at home ○ surprised

3. Who will be in Ricky's race?

○ no one ○ Ricky ○ Nancy and Rita

B. Look at page 155. Write each race name on a paper. Then cut out pictures of things with wheels. Paste each picture on the right paper.

Lesson 12 REVIEW

YOU KNOW

- One thing can make another thing happen.
- The words because and so can be used in a sentence to tell why something happens.
- A writer does not always tell you everything you need to know.

Read the story.

Coyote went looking for some food because he was hungry. He saw Fox eating lunch.

"This is my lucky day, Fox," Coyote said. "I was just wondering what I would have for lunch. Move over!"

Now Fox was very tricky. She said, "Let's have a race to see who gets this lunch."

A. Why did Coyote go looking for food? Write the answer.

____

B. Put a ✓ in front of the answer.

1. What did Coyote think he would eat?

_____ Fox _____ Fox's lunch _____ his own lunch

2. Why did Fox want to have a race?

_____ Fox felt like running.

_____ Fox needed a new lunch.

_____ Fox wanted to trick Coyote.

USING WHAT YOU KNOW

"Good," said Coyote. "I am a very fast runner. I will surely get this lunch."

"We'll see," said Fox. "Let's race beside this wall. You run on this side, and I'll run on the other side. The wall is very high. You will not be able to see me while we are racing. But we will know who the winner is when we reach the other end."

As soon as Fox got to the other side of the wall, she ran to get her sister.

A. Underline the answer.

1. Why did Coyote think he would get the lunch?

He could run very fast. He could eat quickly.

2. Fox and Coyote will not see each other when they run because

the wall is far away the wall is very high

3. Why did Fox run to get her sister?

to help Fox climb the wall to help Fox win the race

B. Read the riddle. Write the answer.

I am an animal with a pointed nose and a bushy tail. I am very clever. In stories, I often play tricks on other animals. What am I? ____________________

Turn your book upside down to see if your answer is right.

fox

WHILE YOU READ

Tip To find out why something happens, think about what happens first. Also use what the writer tells to find out what the writer does not tell. These things will help you understand the story.

Fox said to her sister, "Coyote and I are having a race. Hide at the far end of the wall. I will not really run. Coyote can't see me. He won't know. Then you jump up when he gets near you. He'll think you're me."

That's what they did. Coyote was surprised to see Fox had won the race. "Let's race back," he said. But Fox won again. They kept racing back and forth. Fox kept winning. At last Coyote gave up.

"I guess I'll eat my lunch now," said Fox.

Coyote went away hungrier than before.

AFTER YOU READ

A. Fill in the circle for the answer.

1. Coyote was surprised because Fox
○ ran back ○ won the race ○ ate him

2. Coyote thought Fox's sister was
○ Fox ○ Fox's mother ○ another fox

3. Coyote lost the race because he was
○ hungry ○ too slow ○ tricked

B. Make up a story about how a fox tricked another animal. Tell your story to a friend.

Lesson 13 PREDICTING OUTCOMES / WHAT HAPPENS NEXT

YOU KNOW

- A writer sometimes gives clues about what will happen next in a story.

Read the clues. Then read what happens.

CLUES	Scott was at the beach. He was building a sand castle near the water. He didn't see the big wave coming. It splashed down.
WHAT HAPPENS	The wave knocked down the castle. Scott got all wet.

A. Read the story.

Allie put on her bathing suit. She grabbed a towel and walked onto the sand. She went along until she got to the edge of the water. She dropped her towel and walked into the water.

B. Put a ✓ in front of the answer.

1. What was Allie wearing?

_____ a towel _____ a bathing suit _____ sand

2. Allie walked into the

_____ swings _____ house _____ water

3. What happened next?

_____ Allie took a nap.
_____ Allie went swimming.
_____ Allie filled a pail with sand.

USING WHAT YOU KNOW

Nobody knew it, but Angie didn't like the beach very much. She didn't like the hot sun. She didn't like the sand and salt water.

Every summer Angie and her family visit a different place. Last summer they went to the mountains. Angie liked that trip.

One day Angie's mother said to her, "Guess where we're going this summer, Angie."

"Are we going to the mountains?" she asked.

"No," said Mom. "We're going to the beach!"

To decide what happens next in the story, think about what has already happened. Also think about what the writer tells you about people and things in the story. What you decide should make sense with what you read in the story.

1. Underline the sentence that tells what happened next.

   Angie said, "I think that's a great idea, Mom."

   Angie asked, "Can't we go somewhere else?"

2. Underline the sentences in the story that helped you decide what happened next.

3. What do you think Angie will do at the beach? Write a sentence.

WHILE YOU READ

To decide what happens next, use what you know about people, things, and what has already happened. What you decide should fit with what you read in the story.

Angie was not having much fun at the beach. She sat on a blanket under an umbrella. She read her books and watched the waves.

One day a ball rolled up to her. Angie threw it back to the children who lost it. Then a boy threw the ball back to Angie. Before she knew it, she was playing ball. Soon she was having so much fun she didn't notice they were playing in the water. It felt nice and cool.

At the end of the day, the boy asked Angie, "Will you play ball with us tomorrow?"

AFTER YOU READ

A. Fill in the circle for the answer.

1. When Angie was playing ball, she

○ lost the ball ○ fell down ○ had fun

2. At the end, Angie ______ the beach.

○ liked ○ left ○ watched

3. What will Angie do tomorrow?

○ go swimming ○ read ○ play ball

B. What is your favorite game? Draw a picture of how you would play it at the beach.

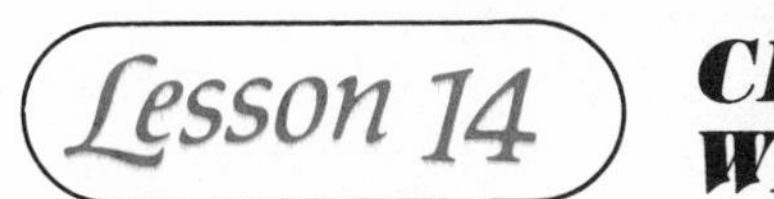

Lesson 14 CHARACTERS / HOW THEY FEEL, WHAT THEY DO

YOU KNOW

- A character is a person or an animal in a story.

Read the story.

Sandy sat on the steps. Tears filled his eyes. His new bike was on the ground. He had tried to ride the bike every day since he got it. But every day he just fell down.

Lou and Gloria rode by on their bikes. Lou shouted, "Come on, Sandy. Just try!"

"I <u>have</u> been trying!" Sandy shouted back. They didn't seem to understand. Didn't they see how hard he was trying?

A. Underline the answer.

1. Who is the story about?
Lou Sandy Gloria

2. What did Sandy want to do?
go to school ride his bike

3. What was Sandy doing every day?
trying to ride playing with his friends

B. Here are some words about bike riding.

easy fast race hard fun slow

Use two or more of the words to write a sentence about riding a bike.

___

USING WHAT YOU KNOW

Sandy got up and kicked the bike. "I'll never learn to ride you!" he thought. Then he saw his big brother Ron coming down the street.

"What's wrong?" asked Ron. "Is the bike too big for you?"

"No," said Sandy. "I just can't ride it." He hung his head and started to cry again.

Ron smiled at Sandy. "Hey there," he said. "You just need to believe you can ride it. I think I can help you, too."

To find out about the characters in the story, think about what they thought, said, and did. The things the characters thought, said, and did can tell you how they felt and why they acted as they did.

Write a word that goes in the sentence.

1. Sandy kicked the bike. He was ______________________.
2. Sandy thought he would never learn to ride.

   He was ______________________.
3. Ron asked, "What's wrong?" He was being ______________.
4. Sandy started to cry. He felt ______________________.
5. Ron said he thought he could help Sandy.

   Ron was being ______________________.

 Character analysis; using a character's thoughts, words, and actions to understand the character's feelings and behaviors

WHILE YOU READ

Tip Think about what the characters in the story think, say, and do. What the characters think, say, and do can tell you how they feel and why they act as they do.

Ron gave Sandy a small shiny stone. "This is a magic stone," Ron said. "Hold the stone tightly and tell yourself you can do what you want to do. Then you can do it."

"Will it really help me?" Sandy asked.

"If you believe in it," Ron said.

Sandy picked up his bike and got on. He held the stone tightly. "I can ride," he thought. He pushed off. The bike shook a bit, but then Sandy was riding down the street.

"I can ride," Sandy shouted. "I CAN RIDE!"

AFTER YOU READ

A. Fill in the circle for the answer.

1. Ron wanted Sandy to be able to
○ hold a stone ○ ride his bike ○ make a wish

2. How did Sandy feel at the end?
○ sad ○ cold ○ happy

3. Sandy ______ the magic stone.
○ lost ○ believed in ○ rode on

B. Read a storybook. Tell a friend what your favorite characters think, say, and do.

Lesson 15 REVIEW

YOU KNOW

- A writer sometimes gives clues about what will happen next in a story.
- A character is a person or an animal in a story.

Read the story. Look for clues about what will happen next.

A farmer and his son were taking their donkey to market. On the way they met a group of girls.

"Look at those silly farmers," one girl said. "They are walking when they could be riding."

"They are right," the farmer said. "One of us should ride on the donkey."

Put a ✓ in front of the answer.

1. Who is the story about?

____ a group of girls ____ a farmer and his son

2. What were the farmer and his son doing?

____ walking to market

____ farming

____ riding a donkey

3. A girl said the farmers were

____ lazy ____ silly ____ happy

4. What happened next?

____ The farmer and his son went home.

____ The farmer's son talked to the girls.

____ The farmer or his son got on the donkey's back.

 Review—predicting outcomes, character analysis; using given information to predict outcomes and understand a character's feelings and behaviors

USING WHAT YOU KNOW

The farmer put his son on the donkey. Then they went on. Soon they met a group of men.

"Just look at that!" one man said. "That lazy boy is riding while his poor father has to walk. Get down, boy! Let your father ride."

The farmer wanted to please. So he took his son off the donkey, and he got on. They went on. Soon they met some women.

"You are mean!" one woman said to the farmer. "That poor boy can hardly keep up with you. You should let him ride, too."

A. Write a word that goes in the sentence.

1. A man told the boy to get down. The man thought the boy was ______________________.

2. The farmer wanted to please the men. The farmer was ______________________.

3. A woman said the boy should ride. She felt the farmer was ______________________.

B. Put a ✓ in front of the sentence that tells what the farmer did next.

____ He got off the donkey and walked.

____ He told his son to get on the donkey.

____ He asked his son to go home.

WHILE YOU READ

Tip Think about what the characters think, say, and do. Use what you know about people, things, and what has already happened in the story to decide what happens next. These things will help you understand the story.

The farmer wanted to please. So his son got on the donkey, too. Soon they met a man.

"That donkey is too small to carry two of you," said the man. "You should carry it!"

The farmer wanted to please. So he and his son got off the donkey, picked it up, and carried it. Everyone they met laughed at the funny sight. The poor donkey was frightened. The farmer and his son couldn't hold on to it!

AFTER YOU READ

A. Fill in the circle for the answer.

1. When they were carrying the donkey, the farmer and his son felt

○ silly ○ bad ○ hungry

2. What happened next?

○ The farmer sold the donkey.
○ The donkey ran away.
○ Everyone helped carry the donkey.

B. Write a name for the story. Then draw a picture that shows your favorite part of the whole story.

Lesson 16 CUMULATIVE REVIEW

Do you remember the first time you ate popcorn? Did you think it was something new? Popcorn is really one of the oldest treats in the world. Native Americans were eating popcorn many hundreds of years ago.

Some Native Americans popped corn by throwing it into a fire and waiting for it to pop out. Other Native Americans popped corn in big clay pots filled with hot sand. Everyone knew you needed heat to make the corn pop.

Some Native Americans did not just eat popcorn. They also wore it. They made long chains of popcorn to wear around their necks.

1. The story is mostly about
- ○ chains
- ○ popcorn
- ○ fires

2. Popcorn is
- ○ something new
- ○ an old treat
- ○ hard to make

3. Who ate popcorn first?
- ○ you
- ○ your grandfather
- ○ Native Americans

4. What made the corn pop?
- ○ heat
- ○ clay pots
- ○ long chains

5. From the story, you know that people have been eating popcorn
- ○ once a week
- ○ only a short time
- ○ for a long time

6. Which sentence best tells about the story?
- ○ It is not true.
- ○ It is about something real.
- ○ It is very funny.

The corn you pop is not the same as the sweet corn you eat right off the cob. Sweet corn has big fat seeds. Popping corn has smaller seeds. The seeds of sweet corn are soft and wet. Popping corn has seeds with hard shells. The wet part of popping corn is inside the hard shell. Heat makes the wet part get bigger. The wet part pushes against the hard shell. Then, POP!

If you have popping corn that won't pop, the seeds may be dried out. Put the seeds in a jar and add a little water. Put the lid on the jar. Then shake the jar every now and then. The corn should be ready to pop in a few days.

7. What kind of seeds does popping corn have?
- ○ big and fat
- ○ small and hard
- ○ soft and wet

8. Popping corn pops because
- ○ heat makes the wet part get bigger
- ○ the hard shell cracks
- ○ the seeds are small and dried out

9. Which sentence tells the main idea of the story?
- ○ Popping corn has small seeds.
- ○ Sweet corn and popping corn are different kinds of corn.
- ○ Sweet corn is the best kind of corn to eat.

10. If popping corn is dried out, it
- ○ will pop in a few days
- ○ is not good to eat
- ○ will not pop

11. What will happen if you heat good popping corn?
- ○ It will dry out.
- ○ It will pop.
- ○ It will get soft.

Val made a treat for the birds. First she made some popcorn. Then she got a piece of thin string. She put the string through a needle and made a big knot at one end. She took a piece of popcorn and pushed the needle through it. Then she moved the popcorn down the string until it hit the knot. She did the same thing with the rest of the popcorn. Soon she had a long chain.

Val went outside and hung the chain of popcorn on a tree.

"That looks nice, Val," Dad said. "Are you having a party?"

"Sort of," said Val. "My friends should be here soon."

In a little while the tree was full of birds. They pulled off the popcorn and ate it up.

"It looks like your friends are having a good time at your party," Dad said. Val and Dad both laughed.

12. Val made a chain of popcorn because she wanted to
- ○ wear something pretty
- ○ put string through a needle
- ○ make a treat for the birds

13. Dad thought Val was
- ○ hungry
- ○ making chains
- ○ having a party

14. How did Val and Dad feel at the end?
- ○ happy
- ○ smart
- ○ scared

15. Val's friends were
- ○ children from school
- ○ the birds
- ○ Dad and Mom

16. From the story, you know that Val
- ○ ate popcorn
- ○ was lonely
- ○ liked birds

FINAL REVIEW

In 1950, park guards in New Mexico found a little bear cub. It had been burned in a forest fire. The guards took care of the cub until it was well again. They named the cub Smokey the Bear. They used the story of Smokey to warn people about the dangers of forest fires.

Smokey is no longer alive. But Smokey's picture is used to remind people to be careful when using fire in a forest.

1. Smokey the Bear was
- ○ a park guard
- ○ lost in the forest
- ○ burned in a forest fire

2. How did the park guards use the story of Smokey?
- ○ to warn people
- ○ to put out fires
- ○ to take care of bears

3. The guards wanted people to know that forest fires
- ○ cook food
- ○ hurt animals
- ○ keep people warm

4. What is the story mostly about?
- ○ bear cubs
- ○ New Mexico
- ○ Smokey the Bear

5. People who see a picture of Smokey will probably
- ○ visit a zoo
- ○ look for bears
- ○ be careful with fire

6. What was Smokey the Bear?
- ○ a toy bear
- ○ a real bear
- ○ a white bear

Sam ran up to his friends. He was smiling. "Look what I found!" he said. He held up a shiny rocket.

Terry cried out, "That's my rocket ship! I lost it in the park yesterday."

"Well, it's mine now," Sam said. "Finders keepers. Losers weepers."

Terry started to cry. "My grandmother just gave me that rocket. It's <u>my</u> rocket ship!" Terry sobbed.

"Hey, Sam! You should give the rocket back," said Barbara.

Sam stood there. He wanted to keep the rocket. He wished he didn't know it belonged to Terry. Then he gave the rocket ship to Terry.

"Here, Terry," Sam said. "I guess I can't keep it if it's really yours."

7. What did Sam find?

○ a ball
○ a friend
○ a rocket ship

8. Who lost the rocket?

○ Sam
○ Terry
○ Barbara

9. How did Terry feel when Sam said, "Finders keepers"?

○ unhappy
○ afraid
○ glad

10. Sam wanted to

○ go to the park
○ keep the rocket
○ give the rocket back

11. The story helps you learn that you should

○ keep everything you find
○ never find things in the park
○ give back things that don't belong to you

They're Calling

They're calling, "Nan,
Come at once."
But I don't answer.
  It's not that I don't hear,
  I'm very sharp of ear,
But I'm not Nan,
I'm a dancer.

They're calling, "Nan,
Go and wash."
But I don't go yet.
  Their voices are quite clear,
  I'm humming but I hear,
But I'm not Nan,
I'm a poet.

They're calling, "Nan,
Come to dinner!"
And I stop humming.
  I seem to hear them clearer,
  Now that dinner's nearer.
Well, just for now I'm Nan,
And I say, "Coming."

–Felice Holman

12. Who is telling the poem?
- ○ Nan
- ○ a dancer
- ○ Nan's mother

13. At first Nan does not answer because she
- ○ is humming
- ○ does not hear
- ○ is pretending to be someone else

14. When does the writer decide to be Nan?
- ○ at bedtime
- ○ at dinner time
- ○ in the morning

15. Why does Nan hear better at the end of the poem?
- ○ She is tired.
- ○ She is dirty.
- ○ She is hungry.

16. What will Nan do next?
- ○ run away
- ○ eat dinner
- ○ play a game

Did you know there are forests in the water? These forests are not made up of trees. They are made up of a kind of seaweed called <u>kelp</u>. A large kelp forest may cover many miles of the sea floor.

Giant kelp is one of the fastest growing plants on earth. It can grow two or more feet in just one day. In a short amount of time, it can grow taller than most trees.

Many sea animals live in a kelp forest. The kelp is their food. It is also a place where they can hide.

People eat kelp, too. They eat it by itself or with other foods. And something that comes from kelp is used in many foods we eat. It is even used in ice cream!

17. The forests in the water are made up of
- ○ food
- ○ trees
- ○ seaweed

18. Sea animals live in a kelp forest because it
- ○ is a pretty place
- ○ is on the sea floor
- ○ feeds and hides them

19. Which best tells what the story is about?
- ○ "Sea Animals"
- ○ "What We Eat"
- ○ "All About Kelp"

20. A giant kelp that is a year old could be
- ○ as big as a fish
- ○ taller than a tree
- ○ shorter than a person

21. From the story, you know that kelp is
- ○ useful
- ○ reused
- ○ unclean

One day Rabbit could not get into his house. Something was in there.

"Who is there?" Rabbit asked.

"I am the Long One," it said. "I am large and scary. This is my house now. Go away!"

Rabbit was afraid, so he went to get help. But the other animals were afraid, too. They would not help Rabbit.

Then Frog came along. "I will help," she said.

"You are too little," said Rabbit. "How can you help?"

"You'll see," said Frog. She went up to Rabbit's house. "Come out of there!" she said.

"Go away!" said the Long One. "This is my house now."

"I will not go away!" said Frog. "I am the Huge One. You'd better come out. You will not like what I can do to you!"

Slowly a long worm came out of Rabbit's house. "Don't let the Huge One get me," it said. "I'll go away."

"We were all afraid of a worm!" said Rabbit. "Why weren't you afraid, Frog?"

"Your house is little," Frog said. "How could something large be in it?"

22. Why couldn't Rabbit get into his house?
- ○ He lost his key.
- ○ The door was closed.
- ○ Something was in there.

23. Frog wasn't afraid because she knew that
- ○ something big could not fit in Rabbit's house
- ○ the other animals would help her
- ○ the Long One was a worm

24. Frog was
- ○ silly
- ○ smart
- ○ worried

25. Which sentence tells the main idea of the story?
- ○ Worms are scary.
- ○ Rabbit was afraid.
- ○ Frog helped Rabbit.